Due monday.

EXERCISE SCIENCE

An Introduction to Health and Physical Education

Student Workbook / Lab Manual

Dan
Kasslach

DEVELOPMENT TEAM FOR EXERCISE SCIENCE

Workbook / Lab Manual

Ted Temertzoglou, *Toronto District School Board*

Paul Challen, *Hamilton Author*

Jamie Nunn, *Hamilton-Wentworth District School Board*

Kim Parkes, *Hamilton-Wentworth District School Board*

Carolyn Temertzoglou, *Conference of Independent Schools*

The textbook *Exercise Science: An Introduction to Health and Physical Education* represents a long-term commitment to the teaching of physical education in Canada. To this end, we have provided this *Student Workbook/Lab Manual,* as well as a Teacher's Manual, and a set of PowerPoint slides. We have made every effort to ensure that these materials integrate closely with the textbook and we would welcome suggestions as to how to make these materials even better in subsequent editions.

Ontario Physical and Health Education Association

The writing and publishing team would like to thank the management and staff at Ophea (the Ontario Physical and Health Education Association) for their support at every stage of this project – from our early discussions about developing a textbook to match the PSE4U curriculum, to their input during the writing and reviewing process, to their endorsement and widespread promotion of the text. Without Ophea's support and assistance, the completion of the textbook and its supporting materials would not have been possible.

EXERCISE SCIENCE

An Introduction to Health and Physical Education

Student Workbook / Lab Manual

Ted Temertzoglou

Paul Challen

Jamie Nunn

Kim Parkes

Carolyn Temertzoglou

**THOMPSON EDUCATIONAL
PUBLISHING, INC.**

Toronto, Ontario

Information on how to obtain copies of this book may be obtained from:
Website: www.thompsonbooks.com
E-mail: hpe@thompsonbooks.com
Telephone: (416) 766-2763
Fax: (416) 766-0398

National Library of Canada Cataloguing in Publication Data

Exercise science : an introduction to health and physical education.
Student workbook/lab manual / Ted Temertzoglou, Paul Challen, Jamie Nunn,
Kim Parkes, Carolyn Temertzoglou.

ISBN 1-55077-133-7
1. Physical education and training – Problems, exercises, etc.
I. Temertzoglou, Ted, 1964- II. Temertzoglou, Ted, 1964- .
Exercise science.

GV341.T35 2003 Suppl. 1   613.7'1   C2003-904666-4

Cover design: Elan Designs, Toronto. *Cover Photos*: Canadian sprinter Donovan Bailey of Canada blasts out of the starting blocks in 100-metre heats at the Olympics in Sydney, Australia, September 22, 2000 (CP PHOTO/Kevin Frayer).
Shot putter, unknown, (TEP archives, Toronto).

Illustrations not otherwise acknowledged have been provided by Bart Vallecoccia, B.Sc. AAM, Medical Illustrator (Toronto) and are copyrighted by him. Illustrations of bones, muscles, and joints were redrawn from illustrations provided courtesy of Bartleby, Inc. from *Henry Gray's Anatomy of the Human Body*. Philadelphia: Lea & Febiger, 1918; © 2000 copyright Bartleby.com, Inc.

Credits: All text and photo references and credits are provided on the appropriate page in the text.
Anatomical illustrations on pages 23, 24, and 47: reprinted by permission of Lippincott Williams & Wilkins (*Anatomy and Physiology Made Incredibly Easy*, Springhouse Corporation, 2001).

The publisher and authors wish to thank David J. Sanderson Ph.D. for his assistance in developing the biomechanics exercises in Section 15. Professor Sanderson is with the UBC Biomechanics Laboratory in the School of Human Kinetics at University of British Columbia.

The publisher and authors also wish to thank the following Grade 12 students from Humberside Collegiate Institute in Toronto: Rowan Thompson, Jeff Claydon, and Kimberlee French. Their photos and video stills appear in the sections on Biomechanics and Motor Learning and Skills Development.

Every reasonable effort has been made to acquire permission for copyrighted materials used in this book and to acknowledge such permissions accurately. Any errors or omissions called to the publisher's attention will be corrected in future printings.
We acknowledge the support of the Government of Canada through the Book Publishing Industry Development Program for our publishing activities. We acknowledge the support of the Government of Ontario through the Ontario Media Development Corporation Book Initiative.

Printed in Canada.
   4 5   08 07 06

Table of Contents

UNIT 3. MOTOR LEARNING AND SKILLS DEVELOPMENT

UNIT 4. THE EVOLUTION OF PHYSICAL ACTIVITY AND SPORT

UNIT 5. SOCIAL ISSUES IN PHYSICAL ACTIVITY AND SPORT

About the Authors

Ted Temertzoglou is co-director of the Birchmount Exceptional Athlete Program (BEAP) for the Toronto District School Board at Birchmount Park Collegiate Institute. He also teaches Anatomy and Physiology for Fitness at Seneca College in Scarborough. He was a member of the writing team for the course profile and support documents for Exercise Science (PSE4U). He was also a contributing writer for the book *Serious Strength Training: Periodization for Building Muscle Power and Mass* by T. Bompa and L. Cornacchia (Human Kinetics, 1998). He serves as an Ophea Master Trainer delivering workshops around the province and was the recipient of CAHPERD's Young Professional award in 2001. Ted resides in Toronto with his wife, Carolyn, and their two children.

Paul Challen has written several non-fiction books on popular culture and sport, including *The Book of Isiah* (1996), a biography of basketball legend Isiah Thomas, and *Gardens of Shame* (2002), an account of the Maple Leaf Gardens sexual abuse case. He earned his B.A. in 1989 from Dartmouth College in New Hampshire, where he was a member of four consecutive Ivy League cross-country championship teams, and his M.A. from Queen's University in Kingston, Ontario, in 1992. He lives with his family in Hamilton, where he coaches soccer and chess.

Jamie Nunn is a Health and Physical Education teacher at Westdale Secondary School in the Hamilton-Wentworth District School Board. Jamie was a member of the provincial course profile writing team for the PSE4U Exercise Science course including the PSE4U additional support material, the Grade 11 Heathly Active Living Education (PPL30) Prior Learning Assessment and Recognition (PLAR) challenge, and the Grade 12 Healthy Active Living Education (PPL40) Exemplar Project. He recently co-authored an article for *Professionally Speaking* magazine entitled "Healthy Bodies, Healthy Minds, Health for Life" (June 2003) and was co-recipient of CAHPERD's Young Professional award in 2003. Jamie serves as an Ophea Master Trainer and is responsible for delivering workshops and assisting other HPE teachers around the province. Now working towards his Masters of Education, Jamie graduated from Queen's University four years ago. He currently resides in Hamilton, Ontario, with his wife, Danielle.

Kim Parkes is a Health and Physical Education teacher at Westdale Secondary School in the Hamilton-Wentworth District School Board. She was a member of the course profile writing team for Exercise Science (PSE4U), the new grade 12 Health and Physical Education curriculum in Ontario, and the PSE4U additional support material. She was co-author of the article "Healthy Bodies, Healthy Minds, Health for Life, published in the June 2003 edition of *Professionally Speaking* magazine. Kim was also a member of the writing team for the Grade 11 Healthy Active Living Education (PPL3O) Prior Learning Assessment and Recognition (PLAR) challenge. She is also involved as an Ophea Master Trainer, delivering workshops across Ontario to promote Health and Physical Education. Kim was the co-recipient of CAHPERD's Young Professional award in 2003, and she coaches girls volleyball and badminton at the high-school level. She holds an Honours B. PHED from Brock University (1997) and a B.Ed from the University of Western Ontario (1998). She resides with her husband in Burlington.

Carolyn Temertzoglou is a Health and Physical Education teacher at Havergal College in Toronto. She was a member of the writing team for the course profile and support documents for Exercise Science (PSE4U), the new Grade 12 Health and Physical Education curriculum in Ontario. She completed her Honours B.A.B.P.H.E. at Queen's University and was a two-sport varsity athlete. She went on to the University of Toronto to earn her Bachelor of Education. She is a former Nike Fit Pro and has led several workshops in the area of aerobics and fitness for Ophea and the Conference of Independent Schools. Carolyn also serves as an Ophea Master Trainer facilitating workshops across the province. She was presented with the OFSAA Leadership in Sport award in 1997 for her contribution to the sport of field hockey. She also enjoys coaching alpine skiing and track and field. She resides in Toronto with her husband, Ted, and their two children.

Introduction

Exercise Science: An Introduction to Health and Physical Education covers an extremely wide range of topics – from anatomy and physiology, to human movement and biomechanics, to social and ethical issues in sport. At first glance, all this may appear daunting. In fact, however, much that is presented in the textbook is in the form of an overview of key concepts and issues. Indeed, as you go through the course, you will likely want to consult other sources in order to deepen your knowledge of particular subjects. Later on, at college or university, you will find that many of these topics are academic sub-disciplines in themselves, with large numbers of research-level books and articles devoted to each of them.

Much like an athlete training to become better at his or her sport or skill, it is possible for you to develop a deeper understanding of the concepts presented in the textbook by engaging in "workouts" that test your knowledge and require you to do further research. You may be asked by your teacher to use the questions and exercises in this workbook as "practice sessions" leading up to the actual "competitions" – the essays and examinations that will be used to calculate your final mark for the course.

With that approach in mind, this Student Workbook/Lab Manual has been divided into sections that correspond to the sections of the textbook. Each section contains the following components designed to test and further your knowledge of the material presented in the text:

- **Learning Objectives**, which outline what you covered in the textbook;

- **Section Quizzes**, which are divided into multiple-choice, short-answer, and essay questions. These question are designed to test your understanding of the central concepts in each section and demand further reflection and assimilation of key principles;

- **Terminology Review**, which will allow you to review the important words, phrases, and concepts presented in each section; and

- **Exercises and Activities**, which encourage you to "go beyond" what you have learned in the textbook and to examine key topics in greater depth by conducting research, engaging in observation sessions, and applying what you have learned.

The Workbook/Lab Manual has been prepared to aid you in your successful progress through the material presented in the textbook. By completing the exercises, you will refine and further your knowledge of exercise science. This, in turn, will provide you with a base from which to pursue the many careers and occupations available in this field. In fact, this Workbook/Lab Manual includes five exercises designed to increase your familiarity with careers that are open to people who have studied exercise science in a number of settings.

Beyond career aspirations, the exercise material in the Student Workbook/Lab Manual is important for another reason. By refining your understanding of the field of exercise science, you will also improve your ability to make significant choices about developing and maintaining a healthy, active lifestyle, and strengthen your role as someone who can impart information about these lifestyle choices to fellow students, parents, relatives, and friends.

By testing your knowledge of this material, your ability to live in a healthy, active way – and to help others to do so – will only increase.

Ted Temertzoglou
Paul Challen
Jamie Nunn
Kim Parkes
Carolyn Temertzoglou

August 2003

UNIT 1

INTRODUCTION TO ANATOMY AND PHYSIOLOGY

Notes

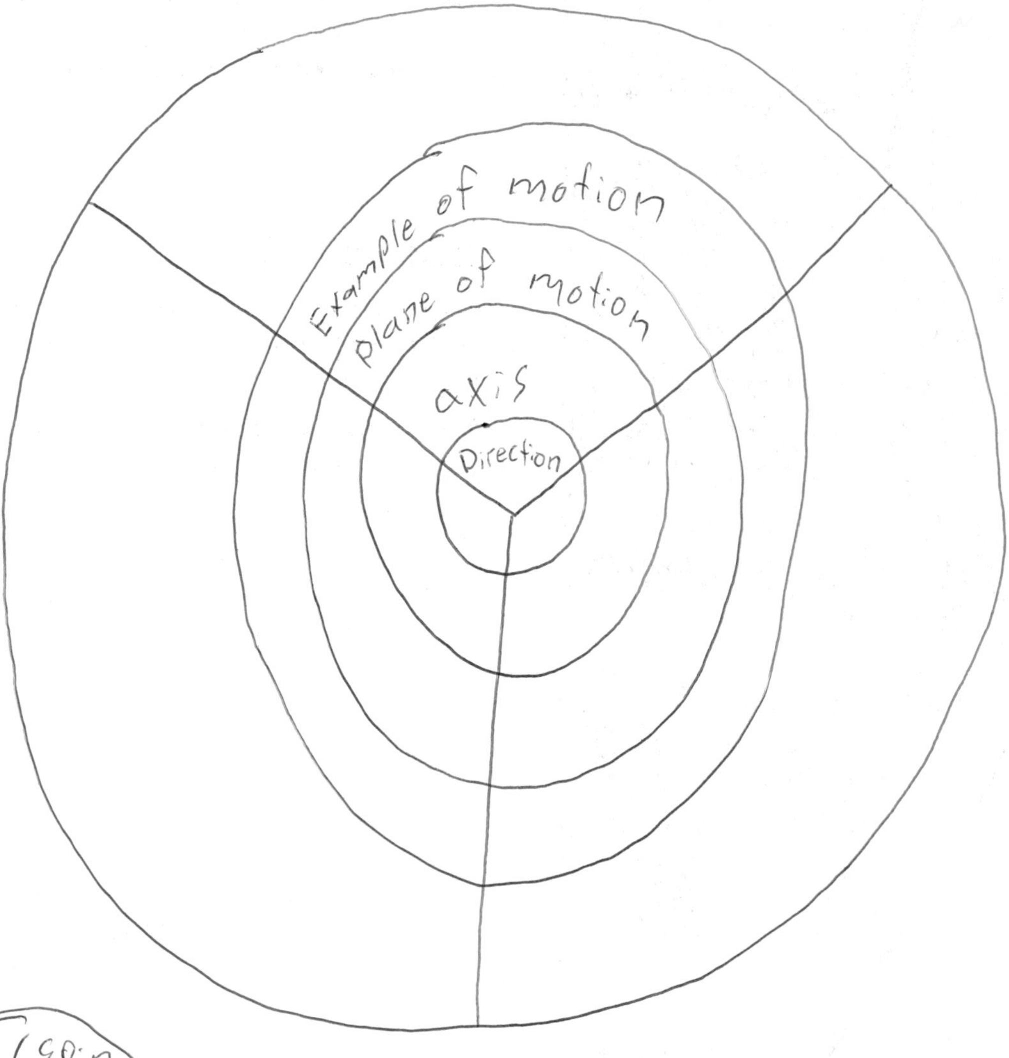
Example of motion
plane of motion
axis
Direction

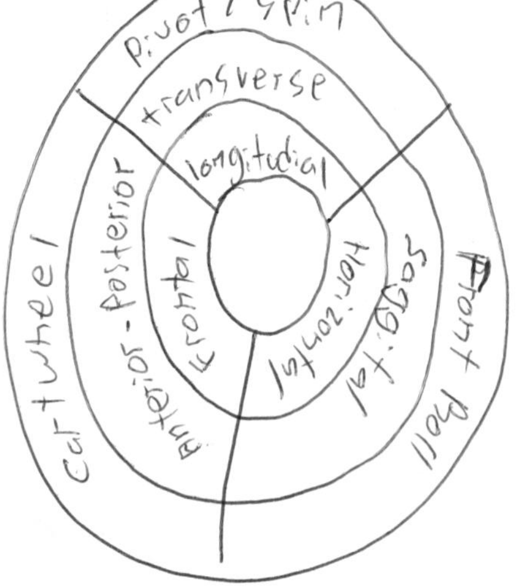
pivot / spin
transverse
longitudial
cartwheel
Anterior-Posterior
Frontal
Horizontal
Sagittal
Front Roll

1

Introduction to Anatomy and Physiology: Principles & Terminology

LEARNING OBJECTIVES

The exercises in this section of the workbook will help to reinforce your knowledge of the following topics covered in the textbook:

- Basic terminology of anatomy and physiology
- The anatomical position
- Anatomical planes
- Anatomical axes
- Basic movements involving joints
- The ten biological systems of the human body

EXERCISE 1.1
Section Quiz

MULTIPLE-CHOICE QUESTIONS

Circle the letter beside the answer that you believe to be correct.

1. **The sagittal plane**
   (a) is perpendicular to the longitudinal axis
   (b) is the only plane that does not form a 90-degree relationship with either axis
   (c) segments the body into a distinct right and left side
   (d) is also known as the "frontal plane"

2. **The frontal plane**
   (a) is perpendicular to the longitudinal axis
   (b) is also known as the "coronal plane"
   (c) segments the body into a distinct right and left side
   (d) can only be seen from the anatomical position

3. **The transverse plane**
   (a) is perpendicular to the longitudinal axis
   (b) is also known as the "antero-posterior plane"
   (c) bisects the body into front and back segments
   (d) involves movements of adduction

4. **From the anatomical position, flexion occurs in the**
   (a) horizontal axis and sagittal plane
   (b) longitudinal axis and transverse plane
   (c) antero-posterior axis and frontal plane
   (d) none of the above

5. **From the anatomical position, extension occurs in the**
   (a) horizontal axis and sagittal plane
   (b) longitudinal axis and transverse plane
   (c) antero-posterior axis and frontal plane
   (d) none of the above

6. **The movement of medial rotation involves**
   (a) the thumb coming into contact with a finger
   (b) moving in a posterior (backward) direction
   (c) inwardly moving the anterior surface of a limb
   (d) pointing your feet out to the side

7. **The movement of supination involves**
   (a) raising the lateral border of the foot
   (b) a combination of flexion, extension, abduction, and adduction
   (c) movement away from the median plane, occurring in the frontal plane
   (d) lateral rotation of the hand and forearm such that the palm faces forward

SHORT-ANSWER QUESTIONS

Briefly answer the following questions in the space provided:

1. What is the distinction between the fields of anatomy and physiology?

2. On what do exercise physiologists concentrate their research?

3. How is the body positioned in the anatomical position?

4. What is the position of the axis of rotation in relation to the plane of movement?

5. Around which axis and through which plane does rotation of extremities and axial rotation of the spine occur?

6. What movement are you performing and which joint are you using when you stand on your "tip-toes"?

ESSAY QUESTIONS

On a separate sheet of paper, develop a 100-word response to the following questions:

1. Explain why it is important for an athlete to have a basic understanding of all anatomical terminology.

2. State the opposite actions of all of the following movements and give an example of where they occur: flexion, abduction, external rotation, pronation, retraction, plantar flexion, and depression.

3. Choose any four of the ten biological systems and summarize their importance to the human body.

EXERCISE 1.2
Terminology Review

DEFINING KEY TERMS

Briefly explain the meaning of the following key terms:

KEY TERM	DEFINITION
Anatomy	A branch of science that deals with the structural organization of living things - how they are "built" and what they consist of.
Physiology	The study of basic processes such as reproduction, growth, and metabolism as they occur within the various systems of the body.
Exercise physiology	A branch of physiology, with the important distinction that exercise physiologists concentrate their research specifically on how the body responds and adapts to the stresses placed on it by exercise.
Anatomical position	Diagrams of the anatomical position portray the the body in an upright, standing position, face and feet pointing forward, with the arms at the side, and forearms fully supinated.
Anatomical planes/axes	-Used to describe how rotation of the muscles and bones take place -Anatomical planes are at right angles to one another - transverse, frontal, and sagittal.
Flexion/extension	-Flexion is bending the joint to reduce the angle between two bones, it occours in the sagittal plane. -extension is straightening a joint to increase the angle. It occurs in the sagittal plane
Abduction/adduction	-Abduction is movement away from the median plane, occurs in the frontal, coronal plane. -Adduction is the movement towards the median plane
Internal/external rotation	-Internal rotation of a limb moves its anterior surface medially -External rotation is the opposite of Internal rotation
Circumduction	-circumduction is a circular motion combining flexion, extension, abduction, and adduction.

Supination/pronation	- Supination is the lateral rotation of the hand and forearm such that the palm faces forward, as in anatomical position
Protraction/retraction	- Protraction is moving in an anterior (forward) direction, (backwards) - retraction is moving in an posterior position.
Dorsiflexion/ plantar flexion	- Dorsiflexion is heel of foot facing ground. - Plantar flexion is toes of foot facing ground.
Eversion/inversion	- Eversion is when the sole of the foo is turned out - Inversion is when the sole of the foot is turned inw
Elevation/depression	- Elevation is raising the body to a superior posit - Depression is the pulling down of the body to a more inferior position
Opposition/reposition	Opposition is the movent of the thumb b touching of fingers. Reposition is when the thumb is returned to anatomic position.

ANATOMICAL PLANES AND ANATOMICAL AXES

Describe the anatomical plane and axis of rotation involved in the following actions:

Movement of the body during the swinging of a bat for a line drive in baseball	
Movement of the body during the back flip of a gymnast	
Movement of the body during a quadruple jump in ice skating	
Movement of the body when bending over to touch the toes	
Movement of the body when performing a cartwheel	

EXERCISE 1.3

The Anatomical Position

The anatomical position is the universally accepted starting point for anatomical description and analysis. The following exercise will help you to become familiar with the features of this position, the axes and planes commonly used to describe human movement, and the terms pertaining to body position.

ANATOMICAL TERMINOLOGY

Label the four illustrations below.

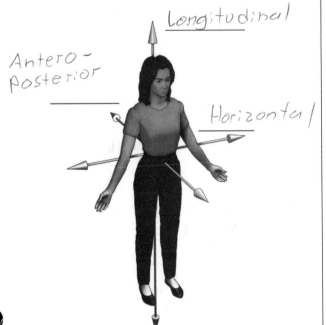

facing
forward

palms
Forward

feet
Apart

The anatomical position

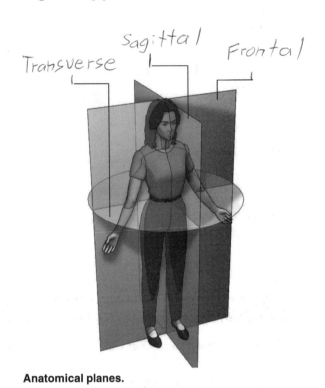

Transverse   Sagittal   Frontal

Anatomical planes.

Longitudinal

Antero-
Posterior

Horizontal

Anatomical axes.

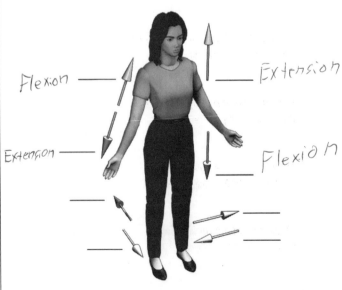

Flexion   Extension

Extension   Flexion

Terms of direction and body position.

EXERCISE 1.4

Movements Involving a Joint

The human body contains a large number of individual joints, and certain groups of them operate in similar ways. In the following exercise, you will be asked to identify several of these basic joint movements.

JOINT MOVEMENTS

Label the movements that occur for each joint in the illustration below.

retraction   Protraction

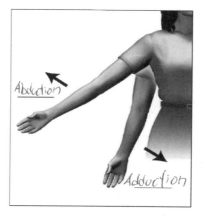

Abduction

Adduction

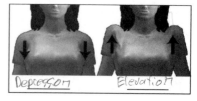

Depression   Elevation

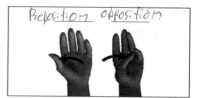

Preposition opposition

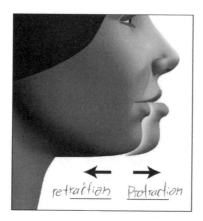

Flexion

Extension

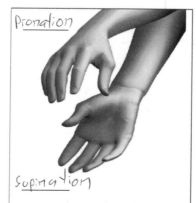

Pronation

Supination

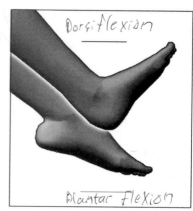

Dorsiflexion

Plantar flexion

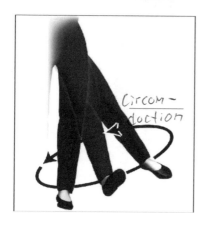

Circum-
duction

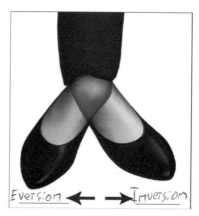

Eversion ←   → Inversion

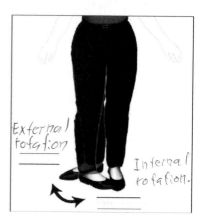

External
rotation

Internal
rotation

Tammy Sutton-Brown, 2002. AP Photo/Rick Havner.

2

The Skeletal System

LEARNING OBJECTIVES

The exercises in this section of the workbook will help to reinforce your knowledge of the following topics covered in the textbook:

- The differences between the human male and female skeletons
- The role and functions of the skeleton in the human body
- The human skeleton's basic structure and composition
- The five types of human bones
- The names and locations of the body's key bones and bone structures
- The concepts of bone landmarks and insertions, and key landmark/insertion sites throughout the body
- The process of ossification and bone formation
- The process of bone remodelling
- Epiphyseal or growth plates of bones
- Bone fractures and their three main categories
- How bones heal
- Bone disease, stress fractures, and the effects of aging on bone

EXERCISE 2.1
Section Quiz

MULTIPLE-CHOICE QUESTIONS

Circle the letter beside the answer that you believe to be correct.

1. **The appendicular skeleton**
   (a) features the sternum as its central aspect
   (b) is the division of the skeleton from which all muscles originate
   (c) can only be seen from the anterior view
   (d) includes the limbs and plays a key role in allowing us to move

2. **The structure found on the ends of bones is**
   (a) periosteum
   (b) diaphysis
   (c) articulating cartilage
   (d) bone marrow

3. **Tendons usually unite and attach to**
   (a) periosteum
   (b) diaphysis
   (c) articulating cartilage
   (d) bone marrow

4. **Which of these muscles originate on the ischial tuberosity?**
   (a) semitendinosus, semifemoris, and biceps femoris
   (b) vastus lateralis, vastus medialis, and rectus femoris
   (c) semitendinosus, semimembranosus, and biceps femoris
   (d) gracilis, pectineus, and adductor brevis

5. **This muscle originates on the anterior inferior iliac spine.**
   (a) iliopsoas
   (b) sartorius
   (c) rectus femoris
   (d) psoas minor

6. **This muscle inserts on the radial tuberosity.**
   (a) coracobrachialis
   (b) brachioradialis
   (c) triceps brachii
   (d) biceps brachii

7. **The os coxae consists of the**
   (a) ilium, pubis, and ischium
   (b) symphysis pubis, obturator foramen, and acetabulum
   (c) anterior superior iliac spine, anterior inferior iliac spine. and sacrum
   (d) Ilium, pubis, and sacrum

SHORT-ANSWER QUESTIONS

Briefly answer the following questions in the space provided:

1. List the five functions of the skeletal system.

2. Why is the axial skeleton so important to body movement?

3. Name the five types of bones and give an example of each.

4. What are the functions of the periosteum, medullary cavity, and bone marrow?

5. Describe the role played by osteoblasts in the formation of compact bone.

6. When is the process known as bone remodelling most active? Why?

7. Name and describe the three kinds of fractures?

8. Who is particularly vulnerable to the condition known as osteoporosis and why?

ESSAY QUESTIONS

On a separate sheet of paper, develop a 100-word response to the following questions:

1. What are some habits and behaviours that can help us to maintain and strengthen our skeletal systems?

2. Explain the processes of bone formation and bone remodelling in the human body.

3. Explain the significance of the presence of an epiphyseal line and epiphyseal plate.

EXERCISE 2.2
Terminology Review

DEFINING KEY TERMS

Briefly explain the meaning of the following key terms:

KEY TERM	DEFINITION
Skeleton	
Axial skeleton	
Appendicular skeleton	
Articulating cartilage	
Periosteum	
Medullary cavity	
Compact bone	
Diaphysis/epiphysis	

Cancellous bone	
Cortex	
Trabeculae	
Ossification	
Bone remodelling	
Epiphyseal plates/lines	
Simple, compound, and comminuted fractures	
Stress fracture	
Osteoporosis	

EXERCISE 2.3

Anatomy of a Long Bone

There are five basic bone types. The most familiar of these is the long bone, examples of which are the femur, the fibula, and tibia. This exercise will help you to gain familiarity with the various parts of the long bone.

LABELS

- ❑ Cartilage
- ❑ Cancellous bone
- ❑ Diaphysis
- ❑ Epiphysis
- ❑ Medullary cavity
- ❑ Periosteum
- ❑ Compact bone

COMPONENTS OF A LONG BONE

Label the main parts of the long bone on the diagram below. Some labels may need to be used more than once.

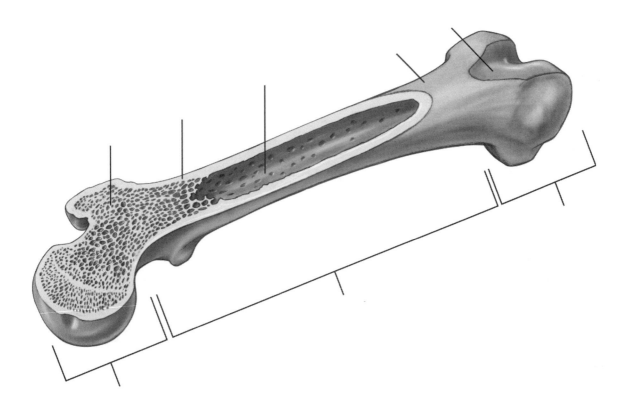

The composition of a long bone.

EXERCISE 2.4

The Body's Key Bones

There are several different types of bone, usually classified with respect to their shape and size. By completing the following exercise, you will become familiar with the names and appearance of these key bone types.

BONE CLASSIFICATION

Label the illustrations below indicating whether each bone is classified as long, short, flat, sesamoid, or irregular. On the following two pages label the body's key bones using the list of labels provided. Some labels may need to be used more than once.

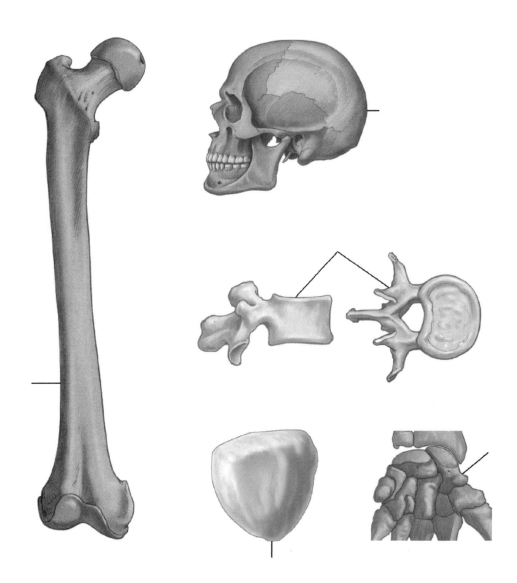

Five types of bones.

The human skeleton (anterior view).

LABELS

- ❑ 12 Ribs (7 True; 3 False; 2 Floating)
- ❑ Carpals
- ❑ Clavicle
- ❑ Costal Cartilage
- ❑ Femur
- ❑ Fibula
- ❑ Frontal Bone
- ❑ Humerus
- ❑ Ilium
- ❑ Mandible
- ❑ Manubrium
- ❑ Metatarsals
- ❑ Maxilla
- ❑ Metacarpals
- ❑ Patella
- ❑ Phalanges (digits)
- ❑ Radius
- ❑ Sacrum
- ❑ Sternum
- ❑ Symphysis Pubis
- ❑ Talus
- ❑ Temporal Bone
- ❑ Tibia
- ❑ Ulna
- ❑ Xiphoid Process
- ❑ Zygomatic Bone

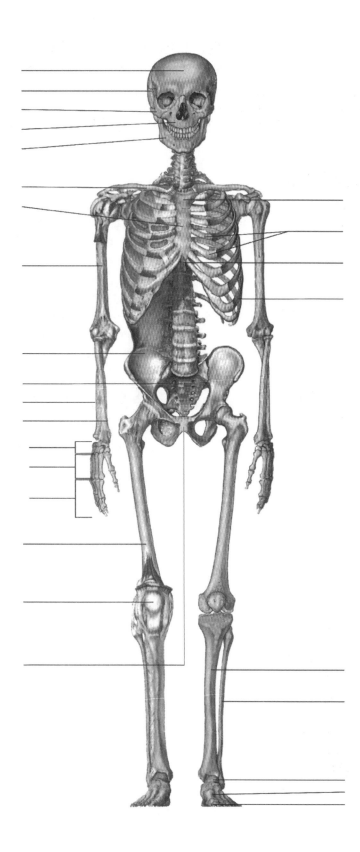

The human skeleton (posterior view).

LABELS

- ❏ Calcaneus
- ❏ Cervical Spine (C1 to C7)
- ❏ Coccyx
- ❏ Femur
- ❏ Fibula
- ❏ Humerus
- ❏ Ilium
- ❏ Lumbar (L1 to L5)
- ❏ Occipital Bone
- ❏ Parietal Bones
- ❏ Sacrum
- ❏ Sagittal Suture
- ❏ Scapula
- ❏ Thoracic Spine (T1 to T12)
- ❏ Tibia

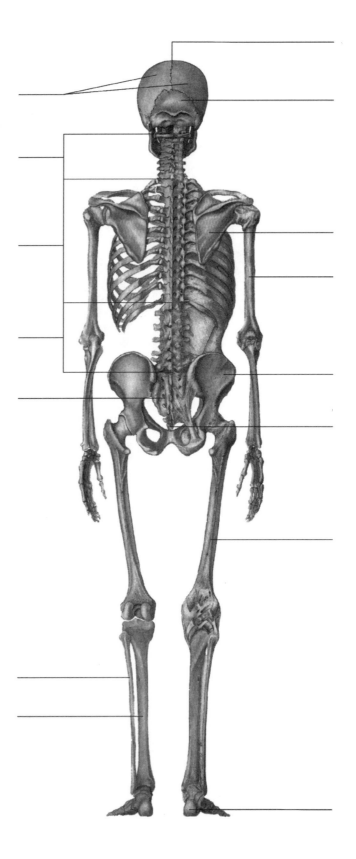

EXERCISE 2.5

Bone Landmarks

The specific locations at which major muscles, ligaments, or other connective tissue attach to bone are known as landmarks. The following exercise will strengthen your understanding of the body's key bones and bone landmarks.

LABELS

- ❑ External auditory meatus
- ❑ Frontal bone
- ❑ Mandible
- ❑ Mastoid process
- ❑ Maxilla
- ❑ Nasal bone
- ❑ Nuchal line
- ❑ Occipital bone
- ❑ Parietal bone
- ❑ Temporal bone
- ❑ Zygomatic bone

BONE LANDMARK LOCATION

Label the various bones and bone landmarks where indicated on the following pages. Some labels may need to be used more than once.

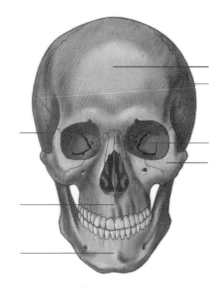

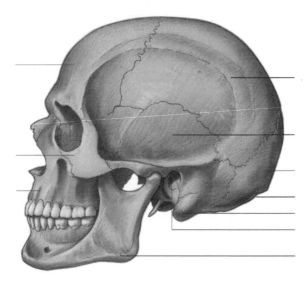

Bones of the skull, anterior and lateral views.

The vertebral column, lateral view.

LABELS

- ❑ Atlas
- ❑ Axis
- ❑ Cervical region
- ❑ Coccyx
- ❑ Fifth lumbar vertebra
- ❑ First lumbar vertebra
- ❑ Intervertebral disk
- ❑ Lumbar region
- ❑ Sacral and coccygeal region
- ❑ Sacrum
- ❑ Seventh cervical vertebra
- ❑ Thoracic region
- ❑ Twelfth thoracic vertebra

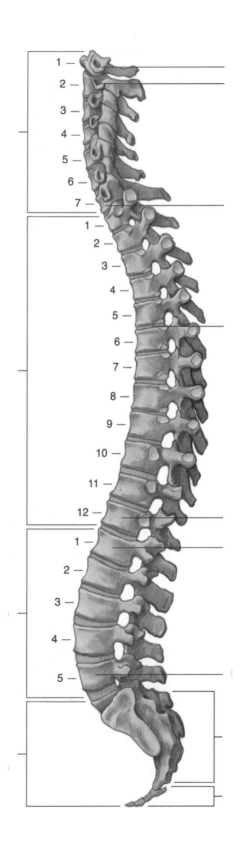

Thoracic cage, anterior and posterior views.

LABELS

☐ Body
☐ Clavicle
☐ First thoracic vertebra
☐ Manubrium
☐ Scapula
☐ Seven true ribs
☐ Sternum
☐ Three false ribs
☐ Two floating ribs
☐ Xiphoid process

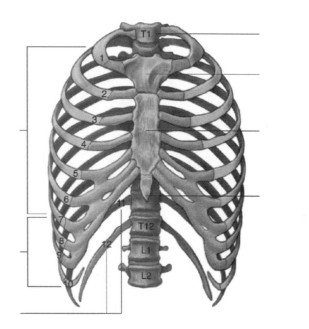

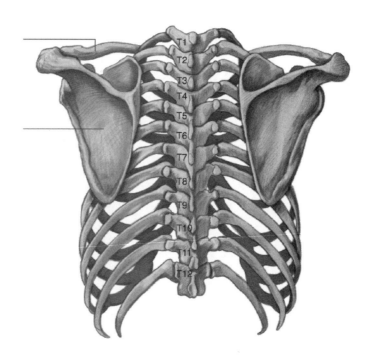

Left scapula (top left), anterior view; left scapula (top right), lateral view; left scapula (bottom), posterior view.

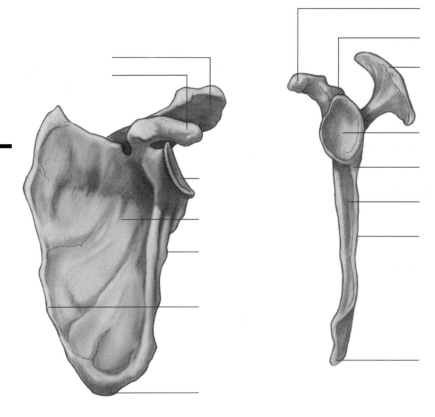

LABELS

- ❑ Acromion process
- ❑ Acromion
- ❑ Coracoid process
- ❑ Glenoid cavity
- ❑ Glenoid fossa
- ❑ Inferior angle
- ❑ Infraglenoid tubercle
- ❑ Infraspinous fossa
- ❑ Lateral border
- ❑ Medial border
- ❑ Scapular notch
- ❑ Scapular spine
- ❑ Subscapular fossa
- ❑ Superior angle
- ❑ Supraglenoid tubercle
- ❑ Supraspinous fossa

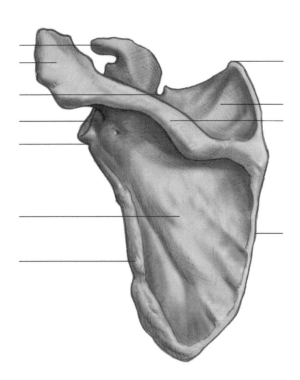

Left humerus, anterior and posterior views.

LABELS

- ❑ Capitulum
- ❑ Coronoid fossa
- ❑ Deltoid tuberosity
- ❑ Greater tubercle
- ❑ Head
- ❑ Intertubercular (bicipital groove)
- ❑ Lateral epicondyle
- ❑ Lesser tubercle
- ❑ Medial epicondyle
- ❑ Olecranon fossa
- ❑ Radial fossa
- ❑ Shaft
- ❑ Trochlea

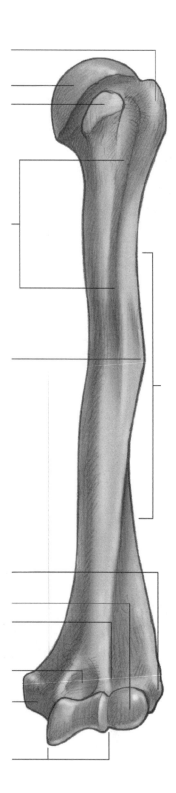

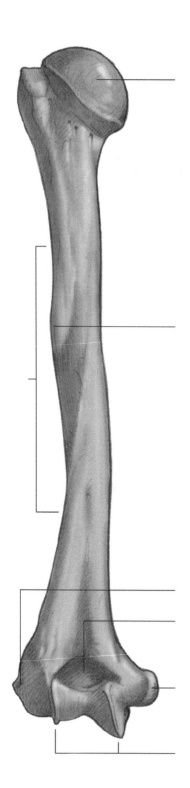

Left ulna and radius, anterior view.

LABELS

- ❑ Coronoid process
- ❑ Head
- ❑ Olecranon
- ❑ Olecranon process
- ❑ Radial notch of ulna
- ❑ Radial tuberosity
- ❑ Radius
- ❑ Styloid process of radius
- ❑ Styloid process of ulna
- ❑ Trochlear (semilunar)
  notch
- ❑ Ulna
- ❑ Ulna tuberosity

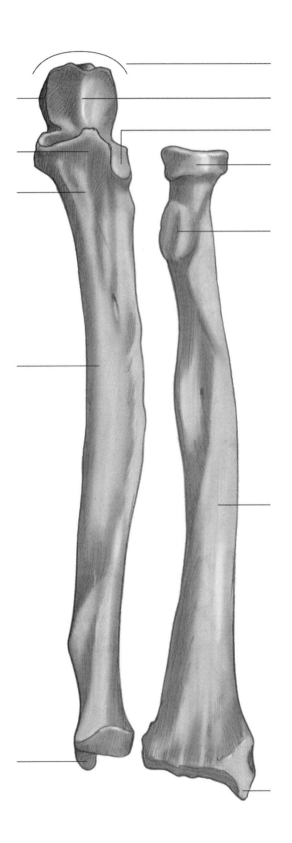

Left hand, anterior view.

LABELS

- ❑ Capitate bone
- ❑ Carpals (distal)
- ❑ Carpals (proximal)
- ❑ Distal phalanx (of finger)
- ❑ Distal phalanx (of thumb)
- ❑ Hamate bone
- ❑ Lunate bone
- ❑ Metacarpals
- ❑ Middle phalanx (of finger)
- ❑ Phalanges (Digits)
- ❑ Pisiform bone
- ❑ Proximal phalanx (of finger)
- ❑ Proximal phalanx (of thumb)
- ❑ Radius
- ❑ Scaphoid bone
- ❑ Sesamoid bone
- ❑ Trapezium bone
- ❑ Trapezoid bone
- ❑ Triquetrum bone
- ❑ Ulna

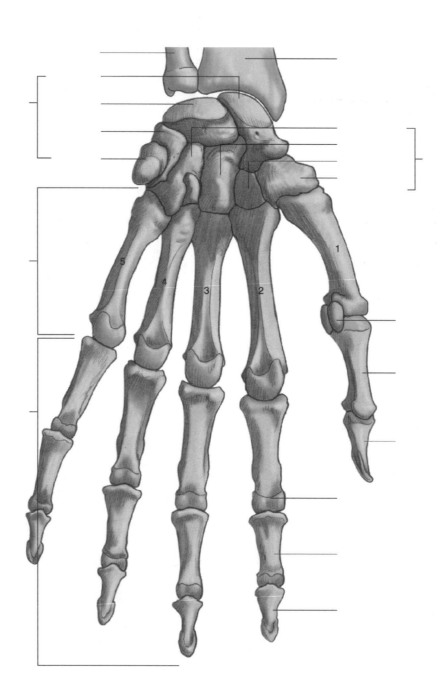

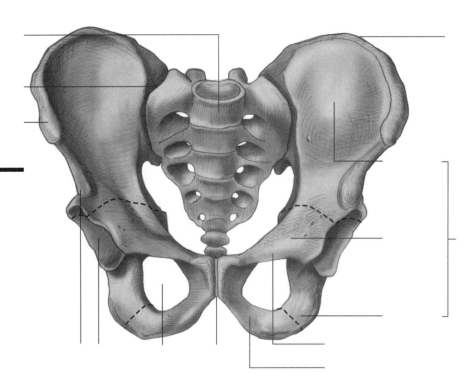

LABELS

- ❑ Acetabulum
- ❑ Anterior inferior iliac spine
- ❑ Anterior superior iliac spine
- ❑ Coccyx
- ❑ Crest of ilium
- ❑ Fifth lumbar verterbra
- ❑ Ilium
- ❑ Inferior ramis of pubis
- ❑ Ischial spine
- ❑ Ischial tuberosity
- ❑ Ischium
- ❑ Obturator foramen
- ❑ Os coxae
- ❑ Posterior inferior iliac spine
- ❑ Posterior superior iliac spine
- ❑ Pubis
- ❑ Sacroiliac joint
- ❑ Sacrum
- ❑ Superior ramis of pubis
- ❑ Symphysis pubis

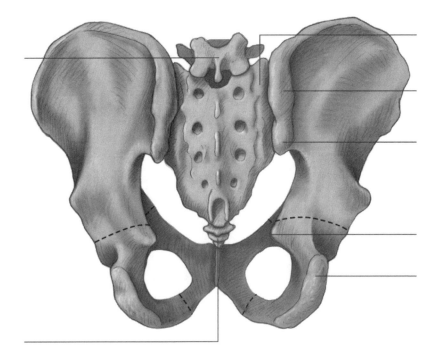

Right femur, anterior and posterior.

LABELS

- ❏ Adductor tubercle
- ❏ Gluteal tuberosity
- ❏ Greater trochanter
- ❏ Head
- ❏ Intercondylar fossa
- ❏ Intertrochanteric crest
- ❏ Intertrochanteric line
- ❏ Lateral condyle
- ❏ Lateral epicondyle
- ❏ Lesser trochanter
- ❏ Linea aspera
- ❏ Medial condyle
- ❏ Medial epicondyle
- ❏ Neck
- ❏ Patellar groove
- ❏ Pectineal line
- ❏ Shaft

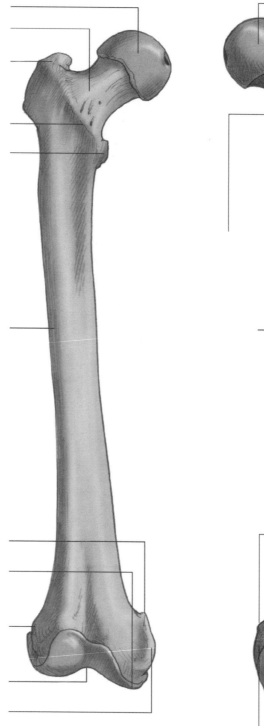

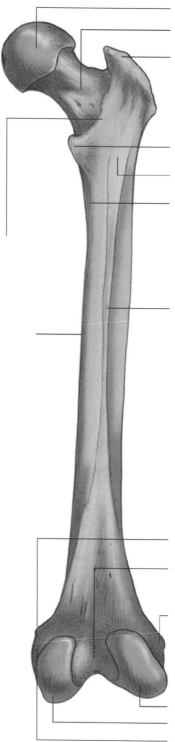

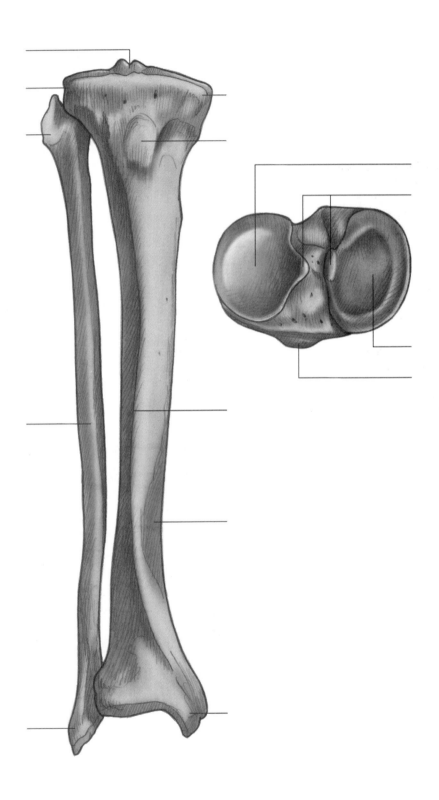

LABELS

❏ Anterior crest
❏ Fibula
❏ Head
❏ Intercondylar eminence
❏ Lateral condyle
❏ Lateral condyle of tibia
❏ Lateral malleolus
❏ Medial condyle
❏ Medial condyle of tibia
❏ Medial malleolus
❏ Tibia
❏ Tibial tuberosity

Right foot, superior view.

LABELS

- ❑ Calcaneus
- ❑ Cuboid
- ❑ Distal phalanx
- ❑ Distal phalanx (of great toe)
- ❑ Intermediate cuneiform
- ❑ Lateral cuneiform
- ❑ Medial cuneiform
- ❑ Metatarsals
- ❑ Middle phalanx
- ❑ Navicular
- ❑ Phalanges (Digits)
- ❑ Promixal phalanx
- ❑ Proximal phalanx (of great toe)
- ❑ Talus
- ❑ Tarsals

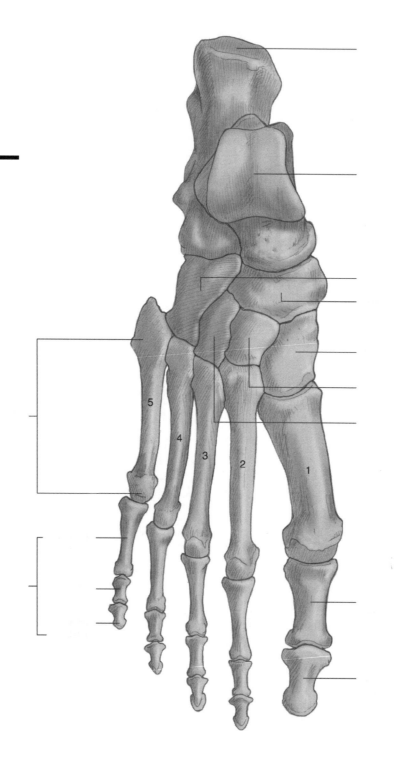

EXERCISE 2.6

Crossword on the Skeletal System

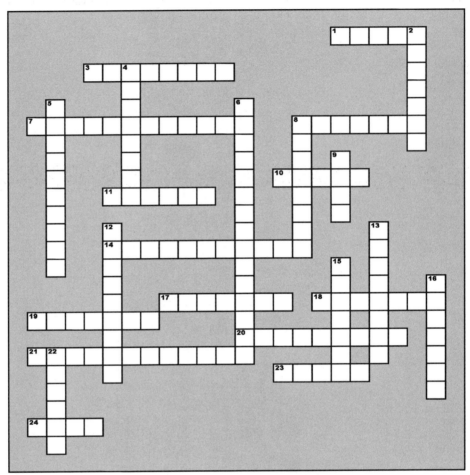

Across

1. The correct anatomical name for the longest bone in the body
3. This type of bone fracture results from a major blow
7. Skeletal division central to human movement
8. As well as protecting vital organs, the skeleton provides this for the body
10. Cells produced in the marrow of bones
11. Girdle connecting the trunk and legs
14. Bone-forming cells
17. The seven bones that make up the ankle
18. Correct anatomical term for the bone that protects the knee
19. Anatomical term for upper arm bone
20. The sphenoid is classified as this type of bone
21. This bone disease affects mainly women
23. Skeletal division composed of the spine, much of the skull, and the rib cage
24. What some of the body's 300-plus bones do over time

Down

2. Disease characterized by defective bone growth
4. Bottom bone of the skull
5. Another name for "growth" plates
6. Muscle that inserts above the styloid process of the radius
8. The Greek word meaning "dried up"
9. Muscles that are centrally located and provide stability and support
12. View of skeleton from the rear
13. Division of the skeleton comprising the lower jaw and branchial arches
15. Bone that has a landmark called the coracoid process
16. The mineral of which bones are primarily composed
22. Key bone that consists of four fused vertebra

EXERCISE 2.7

Landmarks Table — Review Exercise

Bone landmarks are specific locations at which major muscles, ligaments, or other connective tissue attach. The following exercise will further your knowledge of bone landmarks and their location in the body.

BONE LANDMARK REVIEW

Review the illustrations on the previous pages and locate the landmarks indicated below and on the next page. Place a check mark in the box once you have located it. To enhance your learning, colour-code the box and the area of the bone.

Table 2.2: Major bone landmarks and muscle origins and insertions	
Bone	**Important landmarks**
Skull	❑ mastoid process
	❑ nuchal line
Vertebral column	❑ cervical
	❑ thoracic
	❑ lumbar
Sternum	❑ manubrium
	❑ body
	❑ xiphoid process
Clavicle	❑ body
Rib cage	❑ ribs 1-12
Scapula	❑ coracoid process
	❑ acromion process
	❑ supraglenoid tubercle
	❑ infraglenoid tubercle
	❑ spine of scapula
	❑ lateral border
	❑ inferior angle
	❑ superior angle
	❑ medial border
	❑ supraspinous fossa
	❑ infraspinous fossa
	❑ subscapular fossa

Bone	Important landmarks
Humerus	❏ greater tubercle
	❏ lesser tubercle
	❏ intertubercular groove
	❏ deltoid tuberosity
	❏ surface
	❏ medial epicondyle
	❏ lateral epicondyle
Radius	❏ radial tuberosity
	❏ styloid process
	❏ surface
Wrist and hand	❏ surface
	❏ metacarpals
Ulna	❏ surface
	❏ olecranon
	❏ coronoid process
Pelvic girdle	❏ iliac crest
	❏ sacrum
	❏ anterior superior iliac spine
	❏ anterior inferior iliac spine
	❏ pubic crest
	❏ pubis
	❏ ilium
	❏ ischial tuberosity
Femur	❏ surface
	❏ greater trochanter
	❏ lesser trochanter
	❏ medial condyle
	❏ lateral condyle
	❏ adductor tubercle
	❏ linea aspera
Tibia	❏ surface
	❏ medial condyle
	❏ lateral condyle
	❏ tibial tuberosity
Fibula	❏ body
	❏ head
Calcaneus/tarsals	❏ posterior side

Daniel Igali, 2000. CP Photo/COA.

3

The Muscular System

LEARNING OBJECTIVES

The exercises in this section of the workbook will help to reinforce your knowledge of the following topics covered in the textbook:

- The number of muscles in the human body
- The three types of muscles (skeletal, cardiac, and smooth) and their unique role in the muscular system
- Muscle fibres
- The neuromuscular system and the relationship between the muscles and the nervous system
- The motor unit and the concept of "muscle twitch"
- Large and small motor units and the all-or-none principle
- The inward and outward perspectives of the anatomy of skeletal muscles
- How muscles are named, and the basic naming groups within the muscular system
- The ways in which muscles attach to bones
- The concept of "agonist" and "antagonist" muscles
- The origin and insertion of muscles throughout the skeletal system
- Muscular contraction, and the three basic kinds of contraction
- The sliding filament theory of muscle contraction
- How muscle fibre responds to physical training
- The process of excitation-contraction coupling
- The location of key muscles and muscle groups throughout the body
- Ways in which the body's major muscle groups can be exercised, and the role of resistance training as a way of exercising muscles

EXERCISE 3.1
Section Quiz

MULTIPLE-CHOICE QUESTIONS

Circle the letter beside the answer that you believe to be correct.

1. **Which of the following muscles dorsiflexes the ankle?**
   (a) gastrocnemius
   (b) soleus
   (c) gluteus maximus
   (d) tibialis anterior

2. **Which of the following muscles flex the knee?**
   (a) semitendinosus, semimembranosus, and biceps femoris
   (b) vastus lateralis, vastus intermedius, vastus medialis, and rectus femoris
   (c) supraspinatus, infraspinatus, teres minor, and subscapularis
   (d) none of the above

3. **Which of the following muscles originates on the coracoid process?**
   (a) pronator teres
   (b) brachioradialis
   (c) coracobrachialis
   (d) triceps brachii

4. **Which of these muscles insert on the tibial tuberosity?**
   (a) semitendinosus, semifemoris, and biceps femoris
   (b) vastus lateralis, vastus medialis, vastus intermedius, and rectus femoris
   (c) semitendinosus, semimembranosus, and biceps femoris
   (d) gracilis, pectineus, and adductor brevis

5. **Which muscles make up the rotator cuff?**
   (a) trapezius, deltoid, and latissimus dorsi
   (b) biceps brachii, triceps brachii, and rectus abdominis
   (c) supraspinatus, infraspinatus, teres minor, and subscapularis
   (d) iliopsoas, psoas major, and biceps brachii

6. **The primary function of rectus abdominis is**
   (a) trunk elevation
   (b) trunk depression
   (c) trunk extension
   (d) trunk flexion

7. **The anterior muscles of the forearm serve primarily as**
   (a) wrist flexors
   (b) wrist extensors
   (c) elbow extensors
   (d) pronators

SHORT-ANSWER QUESTIONS

Briefly answer the following questions in the space provided:

1. **Which two types of muscle tissue are referred to as being "striated" and why?**

2. **Which parts of the body are surrounded by smooth muscles?**

3. **Explain what the "all-or-none" principle stipulates.**

4. **What lies beneath the endomysium of skeletal muscle and what does it contain?**

5. **What role do myosin and actin play in muscle contraction? What happens to the sarcomere in this process?**

6. **List and describe the five properties of muscle fibres.**

ESSAY QUESTIONS

On a separate sheet of paper, develop a 100-word response to the following questions:

1. **Describe the sliding filament theory of muscle contraction.**

2. **Describe the response of muscle fibres to training and detraining.**

3. **Describe the differences between isotonic, isometric, and isokinetic exercises.**

EXERCISE 3.2
Terminology Review

DEFINING KEY TERMS

Briefly explain the meaning of the following key terms:

KEY TERM	DEFINITION
Muscle tissue	
Tendons	
Skeletal muscles	
Cardiac muscles	
Smooth muscles	
Neuromuscular system	
Muscle twitch	
Motor unit	
Neuromuscular junctions	
All-or-none principle	

Perimysium	
Epimysium	
Endomysium	
Sarcolemma	
Sarcoplasm	
Myofibrils	
Sarcomere	
Adductor muscles	
Abductor muscles	
Extensor muscles	
Flexor muscles	
Agonist muscle	
Antagonist muscle	

Origin and insertion	
Isotonic exercise	
Isometric exercise	
Isokinetic exercise	
Sliding filament theory	
Myosin crossbridges	
Adenosine triphosphate	
Transient/chronic hypertrophy	
Muscle atrophy	
Hyperplasia	
Excitation-contraction coupling	
Transverse tubulae system	
Troponin and tropomyosin	

EXERCISE 3.3

Agonist and Antagonist Muscle Pairs

The agonist muscle is the muscle that is primarily responsible for movement of a body part; the antagonist muscle counteracts the agonist muscle, lengthening when the agonist muscle contracts. This exercise will help you become familiar with opposing muscle pairs in the human body.

MUSCLE PAIRS

Indicate the opposing muscle or muscle group in the table below.

AGONIST	ANTAGONIST
Triceps	
Pectoralis major	
Hamstrings	
Trapezius	
Gluteus maximus	
Erector spinae group	
Gastrocnemius	
Wrist flexors	
Supinator	
Tibialis anterior	
Anterior deltoid	
Latissimus dorsi	
Iliacus	
Adductor magnus	
External obliques	
Infraspinatus	
Rhomboids	
Sternocleidomastoid	

EXERCISE 3.4

The Structure of Skeletal Muscle

The basic unit of skeletal muscle is the individual muscle fibre. This exercise will help you to gain familiarity with how skeletal muscle is constructed.

LABELS

- ❏ Tendon
- ❏ Perimysium
- ❏ Epimysium
- ❏ Endomysium
- ❏ Sarcomere (partially contracted)
- ❏ Actin
- ❏ Muscle fibre
- ❏ Myofibril
- ❏ Myosin
- ❏ Sarcolemma (muscle membrane)
- ❏ Sarcoplasmic reticulum (web-like)
- ❏ Z-line

THE PARTS OF MUSCLE FIBRE

Label the key parts of the muscle and muscle fibre on the diagram below. Some labels may need to be used more than once.

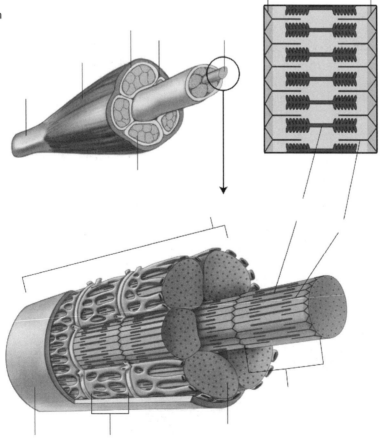

The structure of skeletal muscle.

EXERCISE 3.5

The Neuromuscular System

Muscular contraction is one of the basic elements of human movement. In this exercise, you will enhance your understanding of this process by becoming more familiar with the components of the neuromuscular system and neuromuscular junction.

LABELS

- ❑ Direction of action potential
- ❑ Axon
- ❑ Axon terminal
- ❑ Dendrites
- ❑ Motor neuron
- ❑ Muscle fibres
- ❑ Neuron cell body
- ❑ Neuromuscular junction
- ❑ Receptor
- ❑ Neurotransmitter acelytcholine (ACh)
- ❑ Sarcolemma
- ❑ Synaptic cleft

NEUROMUSCULAR ELEMENTS

Label the illustrations of the neuromuscular system and neuromuscular junction, below.

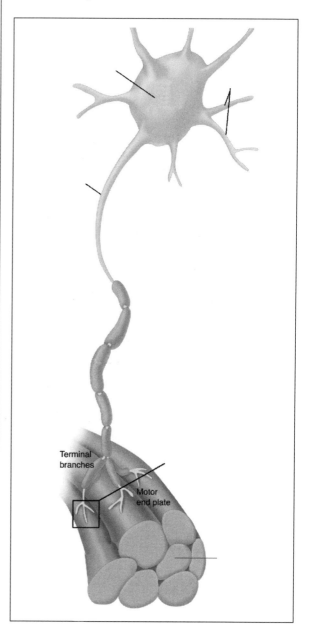

Terminal branches

Motor end plate

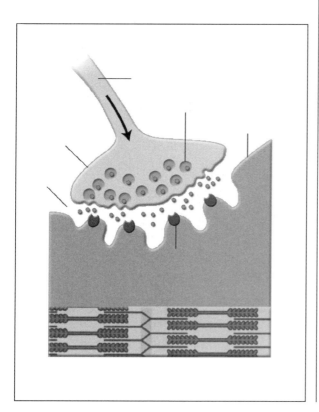

EXERCISE 3.6

Major Muscles of the Human Body

Label the anterior and posterior muscles shown on the illustrations below. At this point you should be familiar with these muscles, thus the labels are not provided.

Anterior view   **Posterior view**

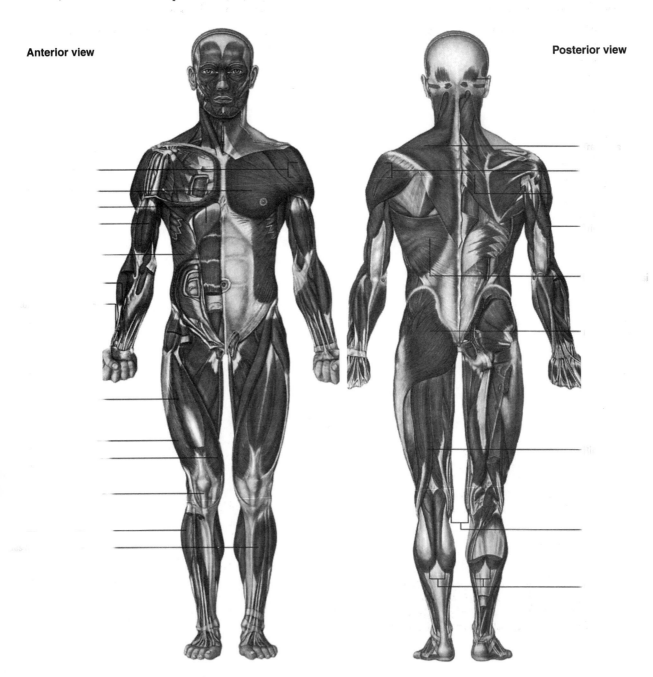

Muscles of the neck, lateral view.
Deep muscles of the back, posterior view.

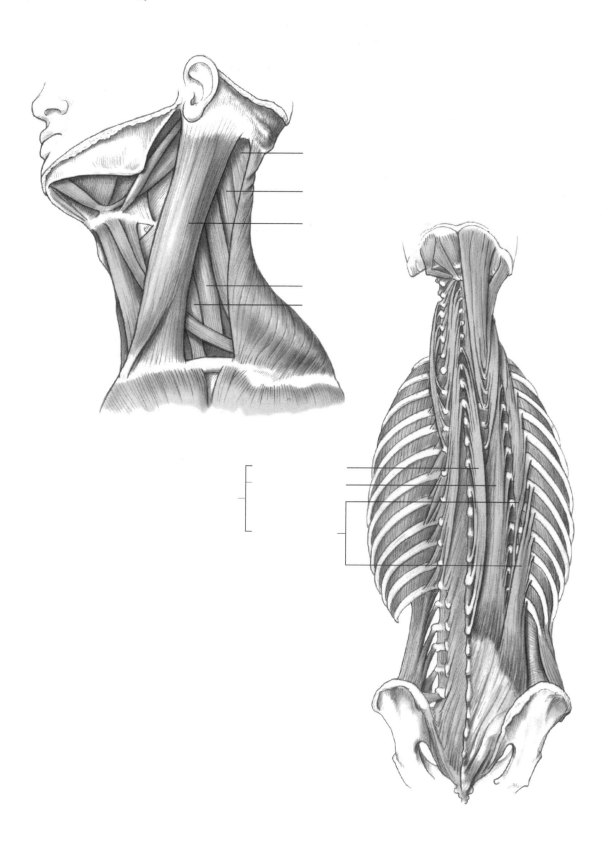

EXERCISE 3.7 – 3.15

Origin, Insertion, and Function

This next series of exercises will help you to gain familiarity with the origin and insertion of major muscles and their function in facilitating movement.

For each of the next nine exercises, complete the following tasks: (1) fill in the chart giving the name of the muscle, its origin, insertion, and function; (2) label the illustrations on the adjacent page; (3) colour-code each muscle name in the chart with the muscle in the illustration. (Your teacher may select only certain muscles to be completed.)

EXERCISE 3.7: MUSCLES OF THE NECK AND VERTEBRAL COLUMN

	ORIGIN	INSERTION	FUNCTION
MUSCLES OF THE NECK			
❑ **STERNOCLEIDOMASTOID** *Sternocleidomastoid is the broad, superficial muscle running upward at each side of the neck.*			
❑ **SPLENIUS** *Splenius runs along the posterior side of the neck and joins the skull with the spine.*			
❑ **SCALENUS ANTERIOR** *One of three scalene muscles on the side of the neck.*			
❑ **SCALENUS MEDIUS** *One of three scalene muscles on the side of the neck.*			
❑ **SEMISPINALIS CAPITIS** *Semispinalis capitis is a deep muscle on the back of the neck that lies below trapezius.*			
DEEP MUSCLES OF THE VERTEBRAL COLUMN			
❑ **SPINALIS** *Spinalis is the most medial of the erector spinae group and is comprised of capitis, cervicis, and thoracis parts.*			
❑ **LONGISSIMUS** *Longissimus is lateral to spinalis, and it also has capitis, cervicis, and thoracis attachments.*			
❑ **ILIOCOSTALIS** *Iliocostalis the most lateral of the erector spinae group.*			

Muscles of the anterior thoracic wall, posterior view.
Muscles of the abdominal wall, lateral view (superficial).

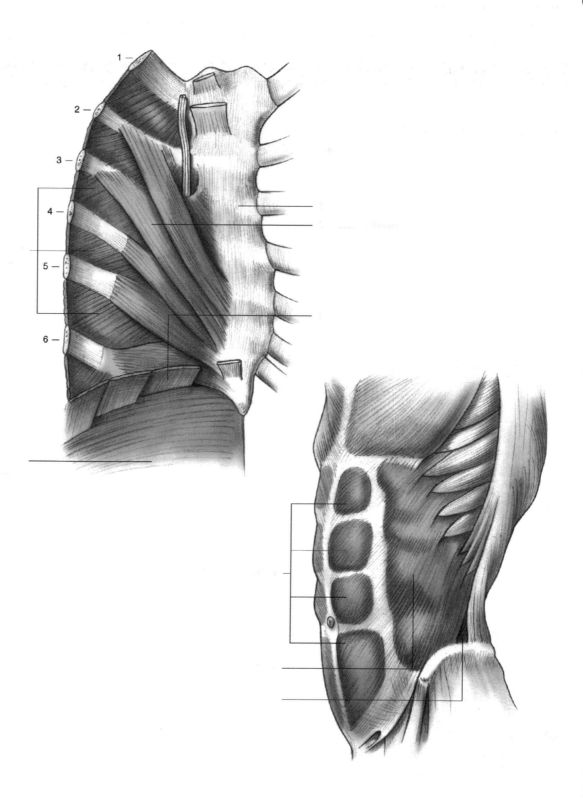

1 —
2 —
3 —
4 —
5 —
6 —

EXERCISE 3.8: MUSCLES OF RESPIRATION AND THE ABDOMEN

The muscles of the thoracic cage are mainly involved with breathing; those of the abdominal wall, with flexion and rotation of the vertebral column. When included with the back muscles, these groups represent the major muscles of the trunk.

	ORIGIN	INSERTION	FUNCTION

MUSCLES OF THE THORACIC CAGE

	ORIGIN	INSERTION	FUNCTION
❑ **THE DIAPHRAGM** *The diaphragm acts as an anatomical border, separating the thoracic and abdominal cavities. Think of it as a plate, in the middle of the thorax held together by a central tendon.*			
❑ **INTERCOSTAL MUSCLES** *The intercostal muscles (external, internal, and the innermost intercostals) are arranged in layers. They are located between each rib, and are often referred to as the breathing muscles.*			
❑ **TRANSVERSUS THORACIS** *Transversus thoracis is a triangular muscle acting on the abdominal wall.*			

MUSCLES OF THE ABDOMEN

❑ **RECTUS ABDOMINIS** *Rectus abdominis is located on each side of a tendinous line (the linea alba) extending from the xiphoid process of the sternum to the pubis. It is also transected horizontally by three "tendinous intersections," giving the abs the classic "washboard" appearance.*			
❑ **EXTERNAL OBLIQUE AND TRANSVERSUS ABDOMINIS** *External oblique is the most external of the abdominal oblique muscles.*			
❑ **QUADRATUS LUMBORUM** *Quadratus lumborum, as its name suggests, has a quadrilateral shape, and it has an attachment site on the lumbar region of the body.*			

Muscles acting on the upper limb, (1) anterior view, (2) posterior view.
Muscles of the rotator cuff, (1) posterior view, (2) anterior view.

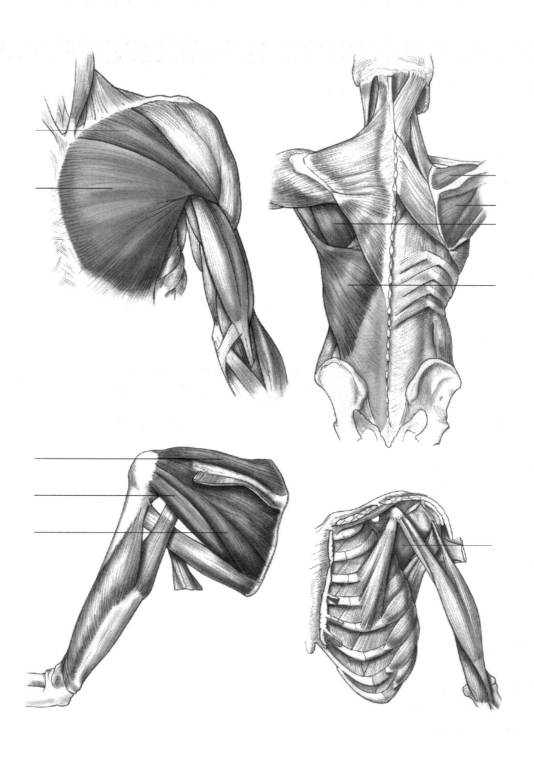

EXERCISE 3.9: MUSCLES OF THE SHOULDER

The muscles that affect the shoulder joint can be grouped into four categories. Two large muscles serve mainly to act on the upper limb of the axial skeleton, and four rotator cuff muscles act directly to stabilize and rotate the joint itself. The other two sets of shoulder muscles (those more directly associated with the scapula) are considered in the following section.

	ORIGIN	INSERTION	FUNCTION

MUSCLES ACTING ON THE UPPER LIMB

These superficial muscles act on the upper limb.

	ORIGIN	INSERTION	FUNCTION
☐ **PECTORALIS MAJOR** *Pectoralis major is the thick muscle covering most of the front of the chest. It is comprised of two sub-regions – the clavicular and sternocostal heads.*			
☐ **LATISSIMUS DORSI** *Latissimus dorsi makes up about a quarter of the back area and is commonly referred to as "lats" or "wings."*			

MUSCLES OF THE ROTATOR CUFF

The rotator cuff (musculotendinous cuff) consists of four muscles that extend from the scapula to the humerus and wrap around the shoulder joint, essentially holding it in place. The group is commonly referred to as the S.I.T.S. or S.S.I.T. muscles (an acronym of the muscle names) because they "sit" on the shoulder girdle. In addition to stabilizing the shoulder joint, the rotator cuff helps to decelerate arm movements (e.g., during a throwing action). If any of the rotator cuff muscles is damaged, due to strain or bad mechanics, the consequences are serious for actions that involve the shoulder and arm.

	ORIGIN	INSERTION	FUNCTION
☐ **SUPRASPINATUS** *Supraspinatus is located above (hence, "supra") the spine of the scapula.*			
☐ **INFRASPINATUS** *Infraspinatus is located below (hence, "infra") the spine of the scapula.*			
☐ **TERES MINOR** *A rotator cuff muscle located below the spine of the scapula.*			
☐ **SUBSCAPULARIS** *Subscapularis is a large triangular muscle, and the only S.I.T.S. muscle located on the anterior surface of the scapula.*			

Muscles of the scapula (1) posterior view, (2) posterior deep view, (3) anterior superficial view, (4) anterior deep view.

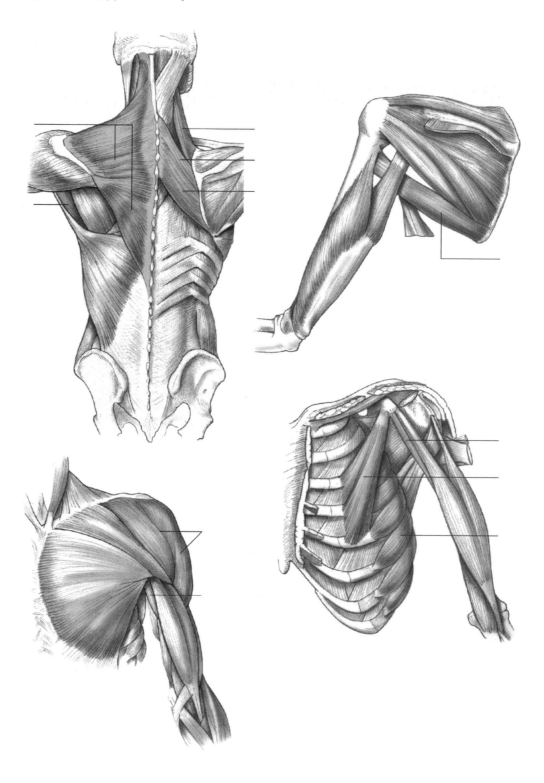

EXERCISE 3.10: MUSCLES THAT ACT ON THE SCAPULA

The scapula facilitates a wide range of movement at the shoulder. Apart from the rotator cuff muscles, the scapular muscles can be grouped into two categories: (1) those anchoring it to the axial skeleton, and (2) those muscles directly acting on the humerus.

	ORIGIN	INSERTION	FUNCTION
MUSCLES THAT POSITION THE SCAPULA			
☐ **TRAPEZIUS** *Trapezius is the large muscle of the upper back that gets its name from its trapezoid-like shape.*			
☐ **RHOMBOID MAJOR AND MINOR** *Rhomboid major and minor lie underneath trapezius. Rhomboid minor is superior to rhomboid major.*			
☐ **LEVATOR SCAPULAE** *Levator scapulae lies along the back and side of the neck and, as its name suggests, raises the scapula.*			
☐ **SERRATUS ANTERIOR** *Serratus anterior is a large muscle that runs along the rib cage, also known as the "boxer's muscle."*			
☐ **PECTORALIS MINOR** *Pectoralis minor is generally classified as a muscle of respiration during sub-maximal and maximal work.*			
SCAPULAR MUSCLES THAT MOVE THE HUMERUS			
☐ **DELTOID** *The deltoid gets its name from its resemblance to the Greek letter delta (hence, it is referred to as the "delts"). It has three heads — anterior, lateral, and posterior.*			
☐ **CORACOBRACHIALIS** *Coracobrachialis is a small muscle that gets its name from its attachments sites.*			
☐ **TERES MAJOR** *Teres major is often confused as one of the rotator cuff muscles.*			

Elbow flexors and extensors, (1) anterior view, (2) posterior view.
Muscles of the forearm, (1) anterior view, (2) posterior view, (3) posterior deep view.

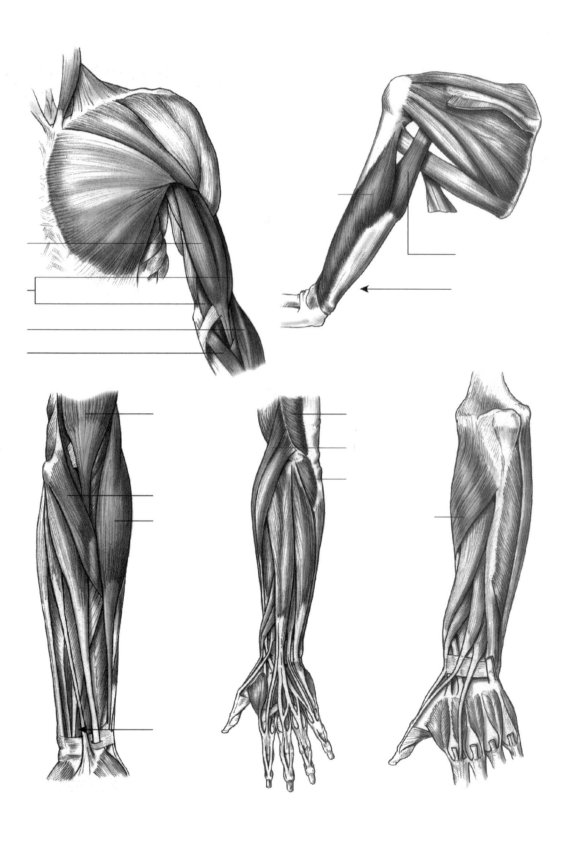

EXERCISE 3.11: MUSCLES OF THE ARM

The muscles of the arm control the movement of the forearm. Two major groups can be distinguished – those muscles that flex and extend the elbow (the elbow flexors and extensors) and those responsible for pronation and supination of the forearm.

	ORIGIN	INSERTION	FUNCTION
ELBOW FLEXORS AND EXTENSORS			
❑ **BICEPS BRACHII ("BICEPS")** *Biceps brachii is the prominent muscle on the front side of the upper arm. Its long head tendon passes within the intertubercular groove.*			
❑ **BRACHIALIS** *Brachialis is sometimes referred to as the lower biceps.*			
❑ **TRICEPS BRACHII** *Triceps brachii has three heads – short, long, and medial. As with the term "biceps" (two heads), "triceps" describes any muscle with three heads or points of origin.*			
❑ **BRACHIORADIALIS** *Brachioradialis gets its name from its attachment to the upper arm (brachium) and the radius (radialis).*			
❑ **ANCONEUS** *Anconeus is a triangular muscle.*			
SUPINATION AND PRONATION OF THE FOREARM			
❑ **PRONATOR QUADRATUS** *Pronator quadratus gets its name from its function and shape.*			
❑ **PRONATOR TERES** *Pronator teres gets its name from its function.*			
❑ **SUPINATOR** *Supinator derives it name from its function.*			

Extrinsic hand muscles, (1) anterior view, (2) posterior view.
Intrinsic hand muscles, anterior view.

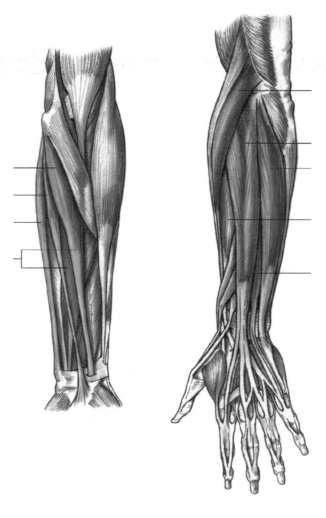

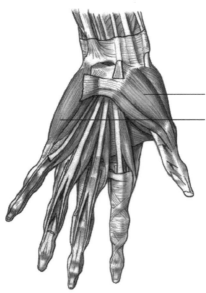

EXERCISE 3.12: MUSCLES OF THE FOREARM AND HAND

The muscles of the forearm (extrinsic hand muscles) are responsible for flexion, extension, abduction, and adduction of the wrist. The intrinsic hand muscles are those contained within the hand itself.

	ORIGIN	INSERTION	FUNCTION
EXTRINSIC HAND MUSCLES			
☐ FLEXOR CARPI RADIALIS			
☐ PALMARIS LONGUS			
☐ FLEXOR CARPI ULNARIS			
☐ FLEXOR DIGITORUM SUPERFICIALIS			
☐ EXTENSOR CARPI RADIALIS LONGUS			
☐ EXTENSOR CARPI RADIALIS BREVIS			
☐ EXTENSOR CARPI ULNARIS			
☐ EXTENSOR DIGITORUM			
☐ EXTENSOR DIGIT MINIMI			
INTRINSIC HAND MUSCLES			
☐ THENAR EMINENCE *Flexor pollicis brevis / Abductor polliicis brevis / Opponens pollicis*			
☐ HYPOTHENAR EMINENCE *Abductor digiti minimi / Flexor digiti minimi brevis / Opponens digiti minimi*			

Muscles of the hip, (1) anterior view, deep; (2) posterior view, deep; (3) anterior adductors, deep view.

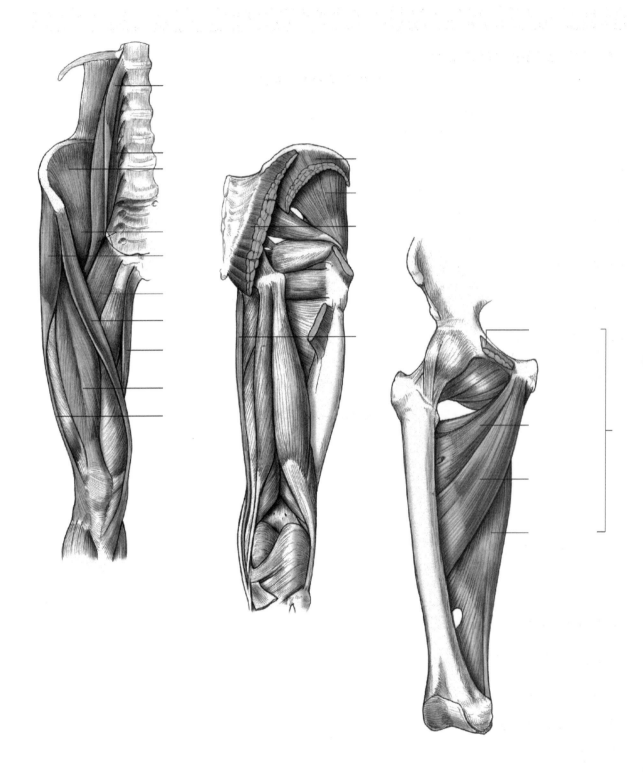

EXERCISE 3.13: MUSCLES OF THE HIP

	ORIGIN	INSERTION	FUNCTION
HIP FLEXORS AND EXTENSORS			
POSTERIOR HIP MUSCLES			
GLUTEUS MAXIMUS Gluteus maximus is the largest, strongest, and most superficial muscle of this group.			
GLUTEUS MEDIUS Gluteus medius lies on top of gluteus minimus.			
GLUTEUS MINIMUS Gluteus minimus is the deepest of this group.			
TENSOR FASCIAE LATAE This muscle lies on the lateral side of the thigh and is enclosed between two layers of the fascia lata (its sheath).			
SARTORIUS Sartorius is a superficial anterior muscle of the thigh. It derives its name from the Latin word sartor meaning "to mend."			
ANTERIOR HIP MUSCLES			
ILIOPSOAS Iliopsoas is a coming together of iliacus and psoas major. • Iliacus • Psoas major			
PSOAS MINOR Psoas minor is present in approximately 40 percent of the human population.			
HIP ADDUCTORS			
ADDUCTOR LONGUS			
ADDUCTOR MAGNUS			
ADDUCTOR BREVIS			
PECTINEUS			
GRACILIS			

Quadriceps and hamstring muscle groups, (1) anterior view, (2) posterior view.

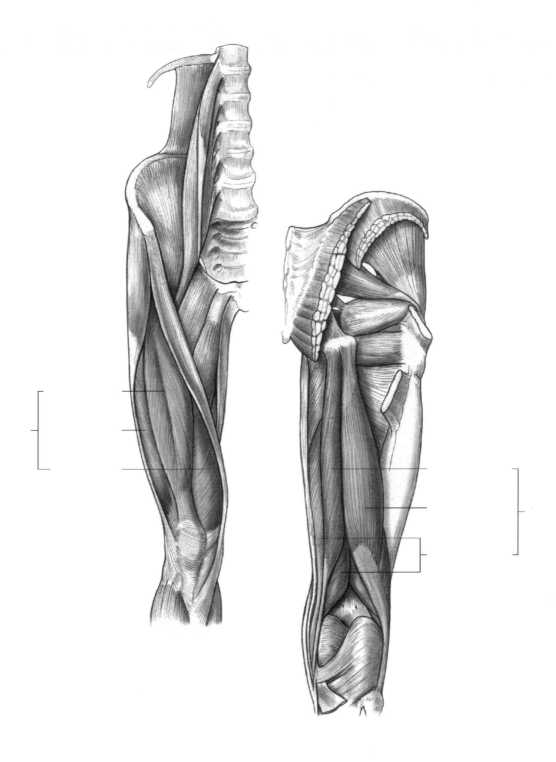

EXERCISE 3.14: MUSCLES OF THE THIGH

	ORIGIN	INSERTION	FUNCTION

ANTERIOR THIGH — QUADRICEPS GROUP

The muscles of the anterior thigh include the quadriceps femoris group. Quadriceps femoris is the large muscle group that covers the front and sides of the thigh. In this group, there are four separate muscles (hence the "quad"): rectus femoris, vastus lateralis, vastus medialis, and vastus intermedius.

	ORIGIN	INSERTION	FUNCTION
❑ RECTUS FEMORIS			
❑ VASTUS LATERALIS			
❑ VASTUS INTERMEDIUS			
❑ VASTUS MEDIALIS			

POSTERIOR THIGH — HAMSTRING GROUP

There are three muscles of the posterior thigh. They are referred to collectively as "the hamstrings." They are: the biceps femoris, the semimembranosus, and semitendinosus.

	ORIGIN	INSERTION	FUNCTION
❑ BICEPS FEMORIS			
❑ SEMIMEMBRANOSUS			
❑ SEMITENDINOSUS			

Extrinsic foot muscles, (1) anterior view, (2) posterior view, deep, (3) posterior deeper view.
Intrinsic foot muscles, plantar views, (1) superficial, (2) intermediate, (3) deep.

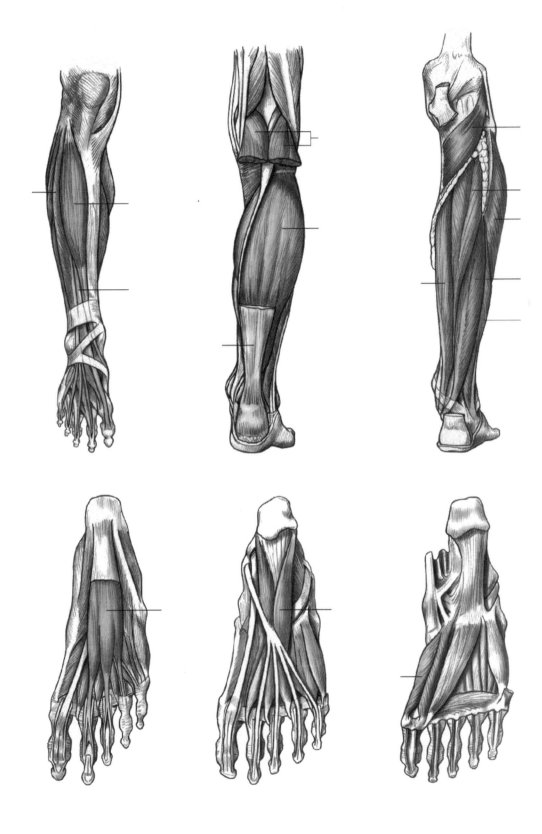

EXERCISE 3.15: MUSCLES OF THE LEG AND FOOT

Anatomically speaking, the "leg" refers to the lower limb below the knee. The muscles of the leg can be categorized into two broad groups, the extrinsic foot muscles and the intrinsic foot muscles.

	ORIGIN	INSERTION	FUNCTION
EXTRINSIC FOOT MUSCLES			
ANTERIOR COMPARTMENT			
❑ EXTENSOR DIGITORUM LONGUS			
❑ EXTENSOR HALLUCIS LONGUS			
❑ TIBIALIS ANTERIOR			
POSTERIOR COMPARTMENT			
❑ GASTROCNEMIUS			
❑ SOLEUS			
❑ FLEXOR DIGITORUM LONGUS			
❑ FLEXOR HALLUCIS LONGUS			
❑ TIBIALIS POSTERIOR			
❑ POPLITEUS			
LATERAL COMPARTMENT			
❑ FIBULARIS BREVIS AND FIBULARIS LONGUS (peroneus brevis and peroneus longus)			
INTRINSIC FOOT MUSCLES			
❑ FLEXOR DIGITORUM BREVIS			
❑ QUADRATUS PLANTAE			
❑ FLEXOR HALLUCIS BREVIS			

EXERCISE 3.16

Excitation-Contraction Coupling

Muscles work essentially by converting chemical energy (ATP) into mechanical energy, a process often referred to as excitation-contraction coupling. The exercise that follows will help you to become familiar with the sequence of events that occur during muscle contraction.

MUSCLE CONTRACTION SEQUENCE

List, in order of occurrence, what happens when you decide to abduct your arm.

1.

2.

3.

4.

5.

6.

7.

8.

9.

10.

11.

4

Joints Mechanics and Joint Injuries

LEARNING OBJECTIVES

The exercises in this section of the workbook will help to reinforce your knowledge of the following topics covered in the textbook:

- The role of joints within the human body
- The structural classification of joints (fibrous, cartilaginous, and synovial)
- Characteristics and types of synovial joints
- Joint tissue and its properties
- Tears, sprains, and pulls
- Tendinitis
- Dislocations and separations
- Cartilage and how it can be damaged
- Stress fractures
- Injury treatment
- The S.H.A.R.P. method of injury diagnosis
- The P.I.E.R. principle of injury treatment
- The properties of the shoulder joint and its common injuries
- The properties of the knee joint and its common injuries
- The properties of the ankle joint and its common injuries

EXERCISE 4.1
Section Quiz

MULTIPLE-CHOICE QUESTIONS

Circle the letter beside the answer that you believe to be correct.

1. **Which of the following best describes a synovial joint?**
   (a) hyaline cartilage is located on the ends of the bones
   (b) it features a joint cavity
   (c) synovial fluid is present
   (d) all of the above

2. **Which of the following synovial joints is a ball and socket?**
   (a) knee joint
   (b) metatarsal joints
   (c) hip joint
   (d) radioulnar joint

3. **Which of the following joints is classified as uni-axial?**
   (a) shoulder joint
   (b) elbow joint
   (c) carpal joints
   (d) thumb joint

4. **Which of the following bone(s) make up the shoulder joint?**
   (a) clavicle
   (b) scapula
   (c) humerus
   (d) all of the above

5. **Which of the following muscles help to stabilize the knee joint on the anterior side?**
   (a) hamstrings
   (b) quadriceps
   (c) gastrocnemius
   (d) gluteus maximus

6. **Tough bands of white, fibrous tissue that allow a certain amount of stretch are called**
   (a) bursae
   (b) ligaments
   (c) tendons
   (d) cartilage

7. **Which of the following injuries is specific to the knee joint?**
   (a) Pott's fracture
   (b) rotator cuff tears
   (c) patellofemoral syndrome
   (d) biceps tendonitis

SHORT-ANSWER QUESTIONS

Briefly answer the following questions in the space provided:

1. **Joints are classified by structure and by function. Name them, giving an example of each type.**

2. **What are the six different types of synovial joints?**

3. **Identify and describe the three types of cartilage.**

4. **List the three common shoulder injuries.**

5. **Distinguish the difference between first-, second-, and third-degree tears, sprains, and pulls.**

6. **What are the three symptoms of a dislocation?**

7. **Why is the knee joint classified more precisely as a modified ellipsoid joint?**

ESSAY QUESTIONS

On a separate sheet of paper, develop a 100-word response to the following questions:

1. **Describe the various properties of body tissue with respect to the likelihood of injury.**

2. **Describe the proper and improper treatment of an injury to a joint.**

3. **Summarize which type of sports or activities tend to cause injury to the ankle and shoulder joints, and why.**

EXERCISE 4.2
Terminology Review

DEFINING KEY TERMS

Briefly explain the meaning of the following key terms:

KEY TERM	DEFINITION
Articulations	
Fibrous joints	
Cartilaginous joints	
Synovial joints	
Gliding (or plane or arthrodial) joints	
Hinge (ginglymus) joints	
Pivot (or trochoid) joints	
Ellipsoid joints	
Saddle joints	
Ball-and-socket (spheroidal) joints	
Ligament	
Tendon	
Vascularity	
Strains, pulls, and tears	

Tendinitis	
Dislocation	
Separations	
Cartilage	
Arthroscopy	
Shin splints	
P.I.E.R. principle	
Biceps tendinitis	
Shoulder separation	
Shoulder dislocation	
Rotator cuff tears	
Knee ligament tears	
Q-angle	
Osgood-Schlatter syndrome	
Patellofemoral syndrome (PFS)	
Inversion sprains	
Eversion sprains	
Pott's Fracture	

EXERCISE 4.3

The Characteristics of a Synovial Joint

Synovial joints are one of the three major joint types. The following exercise is designed to increase your familiarity with the main aspects of this important joint.

LABELS

- ❑ Articular cartilage
- ❑ Blood vessel
- ❑ Bone
- ❑ Bursa
- ❑ Fibrous capsule
- ❑ Fibrous layer
- ❑ Joint capsule
- ❑ Joint cavity (filled with synovial fluid)
- ❑ Membranous layer
- ❑ Nerve
- ❑ Periosteum
- ❑ Synovial membrane
- ❑ Tendon
- ❑ Tendon sheath

SYNOVIAL JOINT COMPOSITION

Label the synovial joint illustration below. (Your teacher may select only certain labels for you to use.)

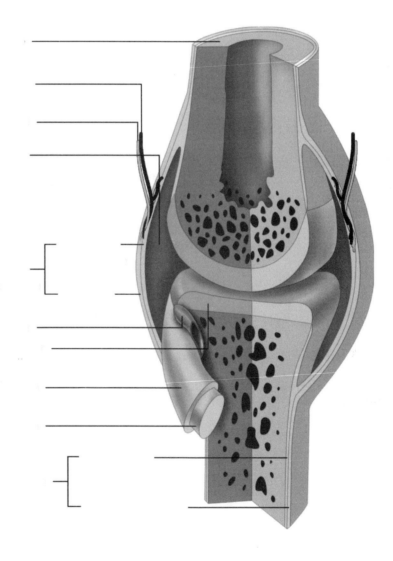

EXERCISE 4.4

Shoulder and Knee Joints

Because of their size and composition, the knees and shoulders are key joints in the human body. The following exercise will test your knowledge of the composition of these joints from a number of anatomical perspectives.

LABELS

- ❑ Acromioclavicular ligament
- ❑ Acromion
- ❑ Clavicle
- ❑ Coracoacromial ligament
- ❑ Coracoclavicular ligament
- ❑ Coracoid process
- ❑ Glenohumeral ligaments and joint capsule
- ❑ Humerus
- ❑ Scapula
- ❑ Tendon of biceps brachii (long head)

JOINT COMPOSITION

Label the main components of the shoulder joint illustrated below, as well as the four anatomical views of the knee joint on the following pages. Some labels may need to be used more than once. (Your teacher may select only certain labels for you to use.)

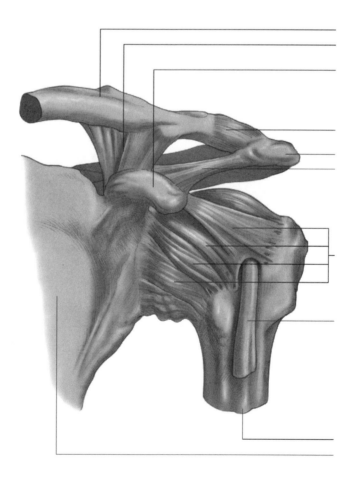

Left shoulder joint, anterior view.

Right knee, anterior and anterior deep views.

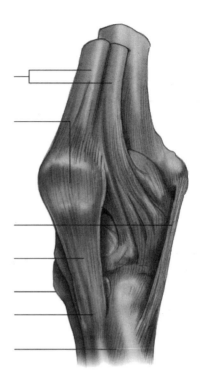

LABELS

- ❑ Anterior cruciate ligament
- ❑ Femur
- ❑ Fibula
- ❑ Lateral (Fibular) collateral ligament removed
- ❑ Lateral condyle
- ❑ Lateral meniscus
- ❑ Medial condyle
- ❑ Medial (Tibial) collateral ligament
- ❑ Medial (Tibial) collateral ligament removed
- ❑ Medial meniscus
- ❑ Patella (wrapped within a tendon – sesamoid bone)
- ❑ Patellar ligament
- ❑ Posterior cruciate ligament
- ❑ Quadriceps tendon (patellar tendon)
- ❑ Tibia
- ❑ Tibial tuberosity

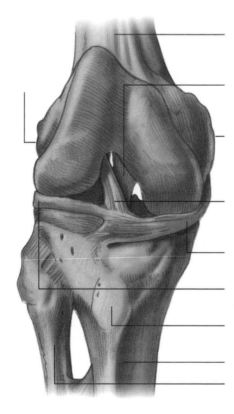

Right knee, posterior view; left knee joint, posterior deep view.

LABELS

- ❏ Adductor magnus tendon
- ❏ Anterior cruciate ligament
- ❏ Femur
- ❏ Fibula
- ❏ Fibular head
- ❏ Lateral (Fibular) collateral ligament
- ❏ Lateral head of gastrocnemius tendon
- ❏ Lateral meniscus
- ❏ Medial (Tibial) collateral ligament
- ❏ Medial head of gastocnemius tendon
- ❏ Medial meniscus
- ❏ Oblique popliteal ligament
- ❏ Popliteal tendon
- ❏ Posterior cruciate
- ❏ Posterior meniscofemoral ligament
- ❏ Sememembranosus tendon
- ❏ Tibia

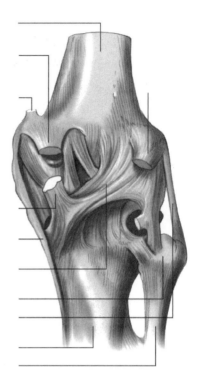

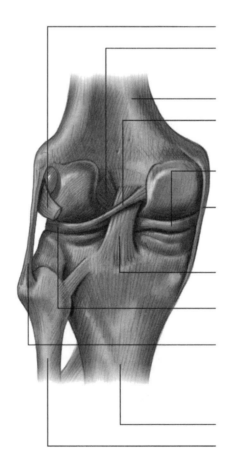

EXERCISE 4.5

Constructing a Model of a Synovial Joint

The components of synovial joints are connected in an intricate and highly functional design. This exercise will increase your understanding of the intricacies of a synovial joint by requiring you to design one of your own.

JOINT CONSTRUCTION

Use the table below to outline the components needed to construct a movable joint of your choice. (You may construct a joint that has already been studied, or select a new one.) Remember, the joint must be able to articulate.

Name(s) of Creator(s)	1. 2. 3.
Name of Joint	
Due Date and Timelines	
Research Sources (e.g., Internet, visit physiotherapy clinic, etc.)	

Materials required to construct the joint

Bones (e.g., paper towel rolls)	
Cartilage (e.g., concave plastic lining from a water bottle)	
Ligaments (e.g., Velcro)	
Tendons (e.g., rubber bands)	
Muscles (e.g., balloons)	

EXERCISE 4.6

Movement at Joints

The muscles and joints are affected by different types of exercises, depending on the type of muscle at work and the particular strains placed on it by each exercise. The following activity will further your knowledge of how various joints respond to different types of muscular exercise.

JOINT ACTIVITY DURING EXERCISE

In the worksheet below, indicate which are the agonist muscles (major muscles) in use, the joints involved, and the type of movement that is produced. (For example, in the bench press, the major muscles are the pectoralis major, anterior deltoid, and triceps brachii; the joints involved are the elbow and shoulder; and the movement produced is elbow extension and medial shoulder rotation and flexion.)

MACHINE	MAJOR MUSCLES	JOINTS INVOLVED	MOVEMENT PRODUCED
Bench Press (example)	pectoralis major, anterior deltoid, and triceps brachii	elbow and shoulder	elbow extension and medial shoulder rotation and flexion
Dumbbell flies			
Lat pull downs			
Shoulder press			
Leg press			
Leg curls			
Military press			
Squats, lunges			
Seated row			
Shoulder shrug			
Triceps extension			
Push-ups			
Crunches			
Power clean			
Arm curls			

Canada Summer Games, London, 2001. CP Photo/Jonathan Hayward.

5
Energy Systems and Muscle Fibre Types

LEARNING OBJECTIVES

The exercises in this section of the workbook will help to reinforce your knowledge of the following topics covered in the textbook:

- The three energy nutrients (proteins, fats and carbohydrates) the body needs
- The definition and role of carbohydrates
- The role of ATP in human energy
- The aerobic and anaerobic energy systems
- The body's three metabolic pathways (ATP-PC, glycolysis, and cellular respiration)
- The role of pyruvate and lactic acid
- The basic functions of the ATP-PC system, or anaerobic alactic system
- The basic functions of the glycolysis, or anaerobic lactic, system
- The basic functions of the aerobic system and the role of cellular respiration
- The lactic acid threshold and the Cori cycle
- How the body derives energy from fats and proteins
- Slow-twitch and fast-twitch muscle fibre types and their roles in human muscular activity
- The function and distribution of Type I, IIA, and IIB muscle fibre types
- The relationship between muscle fibre types and athletic performance

EXERCISE 5.1
Section Quiz

MULTIPLE-CHOICE QUESTIONS

Circle the letter beside the answer that you believe to be correct.

1. **Cellular respiration involves which of the following energy pathways?**
   (a) glycolysis
   (b) electron transport chain
   (c) Krebs cycle
   (d) all of the above

2. **Which energy system uses fatty acids, glucose, and glycogen to make ATP?**
   (a) anaerobic alactic
   (b) anaerobic lactic
   (c) aerobic
   (d) all of the above

3. **Minimum levels of stored ATP and creatine phosphate are limiting factors for this energy system.**
   (a) anaerobic alactic
   (b) anaerobic lactic
   (c) aerobic
   (d) glycolysis

4. **Which of the following is the main product of glycolysis?**
   (a) acetyl CoA
   (b) pyruvate
   (c) ADP
   (d) creatine phosphate

5. **Which of the following sport activities primarily use the ATP-PC system?**
   (a) circuit training
   (b) shot put
   (c) 400-metre sprint
   (d) all of the above

6. **Which energy system(s) does a marathon runner rely heavily upon?**
   (a) ATP-PC
   (b) glycolysis
   (c) cellular respiration
   (d) none of the above

7. **At which level of intensity does a trained individual generally meet their lactate threshold?**
   (a) 100% VO_2max
   (b) 50-60% VO_2max
   (c) 20-30% VO_2max
   (d) 70-80% VO_2 max

SHORT-ANSWER QUESTIONS

Briefly answer the following questions in the space provided:

1. **What is the role of carbohydrates as an energy source?**

2. **What is the anaerobic threshold and how does it differ between untrained and trained individuals?**

3. **What is the role of myoglobin?**

4. **What are the three metabolic pathways to create sufficient energy?**

5. **Describe the importance of the Cori cycle with respect to lactic acid.**

6. **Describe the three separate pathways within cellular respiration.**

ESSAY QUESTIONS

On a separate sheet of paper, develop a 100-word response to the following questions:

1. **Describe the three main energy systems and their limitations.**

2. **During which performance events does the anaerobic lactic system contribute very little energy? Why is this so?**

3. **Describe the role of fats, protein, and carbohydrates in the production of ATP.**

EXERCISE 5.2
Terminology Review

DEFINING KEY TERMS

Briefly explain the meaning of the following key terms:

KEY TERM	DEFINITION
Bioenergetic conversion	
Carbohydrates	
Glycogen	
Metabolism	
Adenosine triphosphate (ATP)	
Anaerobic system	
Aerobic system	
ATP-PC (Anaerobic alactic)	
Glycolysis (Anaerobic lactic)	
Lactic acid	

Cellular respiration (Aerobic)	
Krebs cycle	
Electron transport chain	
Blood lactate threshold/ anaerobic threshold	
Cori cycle	
Fatty acids	
Beta oxidization	
Amino acids	
Myoglobin	
Type I fibre (SO)	
Type IIA fibre (FOG)	
Type IIB fibre (FG)	
Tonic muscles	
Phasic muscles	

EXERCISE 5.3

Three Energy Pathways Compared

There are three basic energy pathways — ATP-PC (the anaerobic alactic system), glycolysis (the anaerobic lactic system), and cellular respiration (the aerobic system). The following exercise will allow you to compare these three pathways.

ENERGY PATHWAY COMPARISON

Fill in the following table based on the criteria provided in the left-hand column.

Three energy pathways compared			
	ATP-PC (ANAEROBIC ALACTIC SYSTEM)	GLYCOLYSIS (ANAEROBIC LACTIC SYSTEM)	CELLULAR RESPIRATION (AEROBIC SYSTEM)
Location of activity			
Energy source			
Uses oxygen or not			
ATP produced			
Duration			
Number of chemical reactions			
By-products			
Basic chemical reaction formula			
Type of activities			
Types of exercise that rely on this system			
Advantages			
Limitation of energy system			
Muscle fibre type recruited			

EXERCISE 5.4

Energy Systems for Various Sports

Every sport or activity involves the use of the three energy systems to a different degree, based on the sport's unique requirements. Some sports or activities rely heavily on one system while others utilize a combination of all three. The exercise below will allow you to explore how specific sporting activities make use of the three energy systems in varying proportions.

SPORT-BY-SPORT COMPARISON

Complete the following chart by indicating the extent (expressed as a percentage or as "highly," "moderately," or "seldom used") to which the four activities listed rely on each of the three energy systems. In the remaining spaces in the left-hand column, choose a sport and provide the same information.

ENERGY SYSTEMS FOR VARIOUS SPORTS

SPORT	ATP-PC (ANAEROBIC ALACTIC SYSTEM)	GLYCOLYSIS (ANAEROBIC LACTIC SYSTEM)	CELLULAR RESPIRATION (AEROBIC SYSTEM)
Weightlifting			
Endurance running			
100-metre sprint			
A 30-second shift in hockey			

6

The Nervous System and the Control of Movement

LEARNING OBJECTIVES

The exercises in this section of the workbook will help to reinforce your knowledge of the following topics covered in the textbook:

- How the nervous system controls human movement
- The two components of the human nervous system: the central nervous system and the peripheral nervous system
- The basic functions of the brain in coordinating human movement, and the key brain areas in which this activity occurs
- The role of the vertebral column and the spinal cord
- The basic functions of the peripheral nervous system, and its division into the autonomic and somatic nervous systems
- The concept of the "reflex arc" and its function in facilitating movement
- Proprioceptors and their function in controlling human movement
- Golgi tendon organs and the tension reflex
- Muscle spindles and their function
- Polysynaptic reflexes and their role in human movement
- The importance of the spinal cord and its potential injuries, including paraplegia and quadriplegia
- Various means of treating spinal cord injuries
- The significance and treatment of head injuries and concussions

EXERCISE 6.1
Section Quiz

MULTIPLE-CHOICE QUESTIONS

Circle the letter beside the answer that you believe to be correct.

1. **Which part of the brain is responsible for coordinating muscle movement and balance?**
   (a) brain stem
   (b) cerebellum
   (c) diencephalon
   (d) limbic system

2. **Which of the following is not an autonomic response of the body to an emergency?**
   (a) increased heart rate
   (b) release of adrenaline
   (c) widening of the blood vessels
   (d) skeletal muscle contraction

3. **Proprioceptors are located in**
   (a) tendons
   (b) muscles
   (c) joints
   (d) all of the above

4. **Which bones are formed by the fusing of bones of the vertebral column?**
   (a) sacrum and coccyx
   (b) thoracic and coccyx
   (c) sacrum and cervical
   (d) thoracic and lumbar

5. **Which vertebrae take the burden of the weight placed on the back?**
   (a) cervical
   (b) thoracic
   (c) lumbar
   (d) tail bone

6. **Which of the following is a symptom of a concussion?**
   (a) memory problems
   (b) fatigue
   (c) dizziness
   (d) all of the above

7. **The somatic nervous system is responsible for**
   (a) preparing the body for emergencies
   (b) muscle movement and balance
   (c) our awareness and adjustment to the external environment
   (d) various automatic functions

8. **The most important function of Golgi tendon organs is**
   (a) to detect changes in muscle length
   (b) to detect tension exerted on muscles
   (c) to house and protect motor neurons
   (d) to prevent the the "knee-jerk" reflex

SHORT-ANSWER QUESTIONS

Briefly answer the following questions in the space provided:

1. **Describe the roles of the autonomic and somatic nervous system.**

2. **Explain the difference between a cerebral reflex and a spinal reflex.**

3. **Describe the difference between a monosynaptic reflex and a polysynaptic reflex.**

4. **What three types of reflex responses indicate problems with portions of the nervous system?**

5. **Identify the three different neurons and describe their different roles.**

6. **Define the terms paraplegic and quadriplegic.**

7. **Who comprises the "rehab team" for people undergoing spinal cord rehabilitation?**

8. **Define a concussion.**

ESSAY QUESTIONS

On a separate sheet of paper, develop a 100-word response to the following questions:

1. **List the main parts of the brain and their function.**

2. **Why do some professional athletes continue to compete despite repeated head injuries?**

3. **Describe the different roles of the tendon organs and muscle spindles of the neuromuscular system.**

EXERCISE 6.2
Terminology Review

DEFINING KEY TERMS

Briefly explain the meaning of the following key terms:

KEY TERM	DEFINITION
Central nervous system	
Peripheral nervous system	
Efferent nerves	
Afferent nerves	
Autonomic nervous system	
Sympathetic system	
Parasympathetic system	
Somatic nervous system	

Reflex arc	
Proprioceptors	
Golgi tendon organs	
Muscle spindles	
Stretch reflex	
Reciprocal inhibition	
Withdrawal reflex	
Crossed-extensor reflex	
Magnetic resonance imaging (MRI)	
Computerized axial tomography (CAT)	
Paraplegia	
Quadriplegia	
Concussion	

EXERCISE 6.3

The Reflex Arc

The reflex arc is the name given to the pathway within the nervous system along which an initial stimulus and a corresponding response message travel. The following exercise will acquaint you with the location of each of its five components.

LABELS

- ❑ Effector organ
- ❑ Interneuron
- ❑ Motor neuron (efferent)
- ❑ Sensory receptor
- ❑ Sensory neuron (afferent)

COMPONENTS OF THE REFLEX ARC

Label the illustration below using the labels on the left and then briefly describe the five components of the reflex arc in the space provided below.

1.

2.

3.

4.

5.

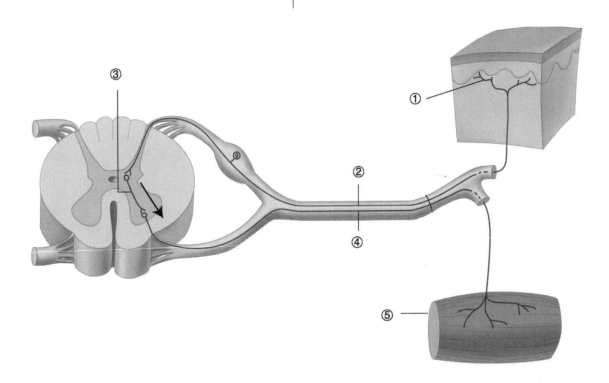

The reflex arc.

EXERCISE 6.4
Golgi Tendon Organs at Work

Golgi tendon organs are a highly specialized proprioceptor that detects increased tension on the tendon. This exercise will allow you to examine the components of the Golgi tendon organ, as well as how it functions through its various stages.

GOLGI TENDON ORGANS

The illustration below shows a tension reflex action involving the Golgi tendon organ. Making reference to the components already labelled on the illustration, list and describe the various stages of this reflex action.

1.

2.

3.

4.

5.

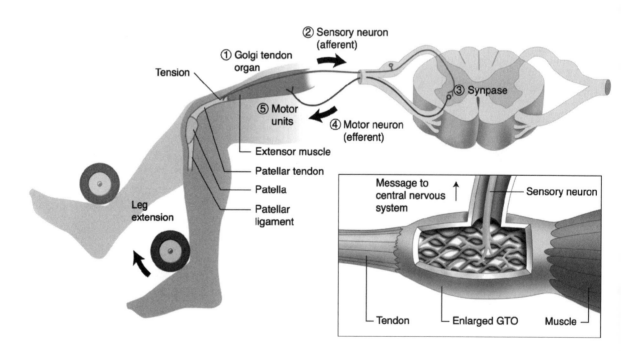

Golgi tendon organ (tension detector).

EXERCISE 6.5

Polysynaptic Reflexes

In more complicated reflex actions - often called polysynaptic reflexes — one or more interneurons are involved. This type of reflex can also involve the presence of a compensation response in an opposing limb. In the exercise that follows, you will study the components and stages of this type of reflex, as well as the elements of the compensation response.

COMPONENTS OF THE POLYSYNAPTIC RESPONSE

The illustration below outlines the actions involved in the reflex withdrawal from a painful object touching the skin. The illustration also shows the possibility of a compensation response in an opposing limb. Making reference to the components already labelled on the illustration, list and describe the various stages of this more complex reflex action.

1.

2.

3.

4.

5.

6.

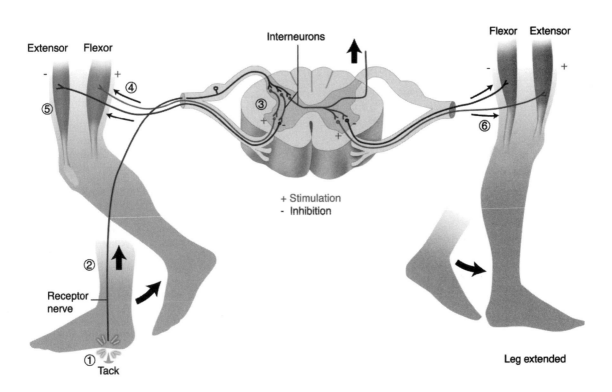

The stretch reflex.

EXERCISE 6.6

Athletes with Spinal Cord Injuries

Paraplegia and quadriplegia are two common spinal cord injuries. Despite having suffered these injuries, many athletes continue to compete in sport and participate in physical activity. The following exercise will allow you to research several outstanding athletes who have overcome spinal cord injuries to excel at sports.

DISABLED SPORT STARS

Complete the following table with as much information as possible on four more athletes – Canadian or international – who have suffered spinal cord injuries but still compete successfully in sport. Try to include athletes from as many sports as possible – both male and female. Use the Internet, magazines, newspapers, books, or videos to complete your research.

One entry – using the material on Rick Hansen found on page 99 of the text – has been completed to provide you with an example of some of the research material needed to complete the chart.

ATHLETE	CAUSE OF SPINAL CORD INJURIES	RESULT OF INJURIES	SPORT(S) COMPETED IN AFTER INJURIES	ACHIEVEMENTS
1. Rick Hansen	Motor vehicle accident	Paraplegia — loss of ability to walk	Track events Road races (i.e., marathons) Tennis Basketball Volleyball	Co-author of 2 books; Multiple marathon winner and world champion in track; Raised millions of dollars for spinal cord research with "Man in Motion" tour
2.				
3.				
4.				
5.				

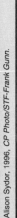
Alison Sydor, 1996, CP Photo/STF-Frank Gunn.

7

The Cardiovascular and Respiratory Systems

LEARNING OBJECTIVES

The exercises in this section of the workbook will help to reinforce your knowledge of the following topics covered in the textbook:

- The basic function and structure of the cardiovascular system
- How blood flows through the heart
- The heart's contractions and electrical "excitations"
- The role of arteries, arterioles, capillaries, veins, and blood within the cardiovascular system
- The cardiovascular system's response to exercise, including the concepts of cardiac output, blood pressure, and blood flow distribution
- The effects of training on the cardiovascular system
- Cardiovascular disease, its causes, risks, and cures
- The basic function and structure of the respiratory system and its importance to the body's overall function
- The two basic zones (conductive and respiratory) of the overall respiratory system
- Ventilation and its controls within the respiratory system
- The body's system of oxygen transport, including carbon dioxide transport, ventilation, and the regulation of blood pH
- Respiratory dynamics, including pulmonary ventilation, external respiration, internal respiration, and adaptations to training
- Oxygen consumption and the concept of VO_2max
- Oxygen deficit and excess post-exercise oxygen consumption (EPOC)

EXERCISE 7.1
Section Quiz

MULTIPLE-CHOICE QUESTIONS

Circle the letter beside the answer that you believe to be correct.

1. **Which of the following blood vessels drains the head, neck, and arms?**
   (a) pulmonary artery
   (b) inferior vena cava
   (c) superior vena cava
   (d) aorta

2. **Which mechanism is responsible for bringing blood back to the lungs and thorax?**
   (a) respiratory pump
   (b) muscle pump
   (c) gravity
   (d) cardiac pump

3. **Cardiac output is equal to which of the following?**
   (a) heart rate x breathing rate
   (b) heart rate x stroke volume
   (c) resting heart rate
   (d) ventricular systole

4. **Which of the following blood vessels carries deoxygenated blood?**
   (a) pulmonary vein
   (b) coronary arteries
   (c) aorta
   (d) pulmonary artery

5. **The mitral valve is located between the**
   (a) right ventricle and pulmonary artery
   (b) left ventricle and aorta
   (c) left atrium and left ventricle
   (d) right atrium and right ventricle

6. **The respiratory zone is composed of the**
   (a) pharynx, trachea, and respiratory bronchioles
   (b) mouth, nose, bronchi, and alveolar sacs
   (c) trachea, bronchi, bronchioles, and alveolar ducts
   (d) respiratory bronchioles, alveolar ducts, and alveolar sacs

7. **Which phase does the QRS complex represent on an electrocardiogram?**
   (a) ventricular depolarization
   (b) atrial depolarization
   (c) ventricular repolarization
   (d) all of the above

8. **Which of the following remains unaffected with respect to blood distribution during exercise?**
   (a) the brain
   (b) the digestive system
   (c) skeletal muscle
   (d) skin

SHORT-ANSWER QUESTIONS

Briefly answer the following questions in the space provided:

1. **What are the three mechanisms that assist in venous return?**

2. **Describe the difference between arteries and veins.**

3. **Of what is blood composed?**

4. **What is hypertension?**

5. **What are the characteristics of an athlete's heart?**

6. **What does a-vO$_2$ difference represent?**

7. **How are active recovery methods more beneficial with respect to anaerobic lactic training?**

ESSAY QUESTIONS

On a separate sheet of paper, develop a 100-word response to the following questions:

1. **Describe the phenomenon known as cardiovascular drift that occurs during prolonged exercise.**

2. **Describe several risk factors that may lead to coronary heart disease.**

3. **Outline the pathway of an oxygen molecule from external respiration to a working quadriceps muscle and the pathway of a carbon dioxide molecule from the quadriceps to external respiration.**

EXERCISE 7.2
Terminology Review

DEFINING KEY TERMS

Briefly explain the meaning of the following key terms:

KEY TERM	DEFINITION
Pulmonary/systemic circulation	
Oxygenated/deoxygenated blood	
Arteries/veins	
Myocardium	
Sinoatrial node (SA node)	
Atrioventricular node (AV node)	
Atrioventricular bundle	
Purkinje fibres	
Electrocardiogram (ECG)	
Coronary arteries/veins	
Capillaries	
Cardiac cycle	

Systolic/diastolic blood pressure	
Vascular system	
Skeletal muscle pump	
Thoracic pump	
Red/white blood cells	
Hemoglobin	
Platelets	
Cardiac output (Q)	
Stroke volume (SV)	
Frank-Starling Law	
Ejection fraction (EF)	
Heart rate (HR)	
Blood pressure	
Hypertension	
Bradycardia	
Cardiovascular disease	

External/internal/cellular respiration	
Conductive/respiratory zones	
Alveoli (alveolar sacs)	
Diaphragm	
Ventilation (V_E)	
Tidal volume (T_v)	
Respiratory frequency (f)	
Respiratory control centres	
Static/dynamic lung volumes	
Gas exchange	
Diffusion	
Partial pressures	
Diffusion pathway	
Henry's Law	
Oxygen transport	
Blood pH	

a-vO₂ diff	
Asthma	
Chronic obstructive pulmonary disease (COPD)	
Oxygen consumption (VO₂)	
Maximal rate of oxygen consumption (VO₂max)	
Respiratory exchange ratio	
Ventilatory threshold	
Lactic acid	
Lactate threshold	
Onset of blood lactate accumulation (OBLA)	
Oxygen deficit	
Excess post-exercise oxygen consumption (EPOC)	
Hyperbaric oxygen therapy	
Passive/active recovery techniques	

Internal Anatomy of the Heart

The structure of the heart is very complex, especially when viewed from the interior perspective. The following exercise will help you to become more familiar with many of the heart's key internal components.

LABELS

- ❑ Aorta
- ❑ Aortic semilunar valve
- ❑ Bicuspid (mitral) valve
- ❑ Chordae tendinae
- ❑ Inferior vena cava
- ❑ Interventricular septum
- ❑ Left atrium
- ❑ Left pulmonary artery
- ❑ Left pulmonary veins
- ❑ Left ventricle
- ❑ Papillary muscles
- ❑ Pulmonary semilunar valve
- ❑ Right atrium
- ❑ Right pulmonary artery
- ❑ Right pulmonary veins
- ❑ Right ventricle
- ❑ Superior vena cava
- ❑ Thoracic aorta (descending)
- ❑ Tricuspid valve

THE HEART'S INTERNAL STRUCTURE

Label the illustration of the heart below. Using a blue pencil crayon to signify deoxygenated blood and a red pencil crayon to signify oxygenated blood, colour parts of the heart and the arrows to indicate the circulation of oxygenated and deoxygenated blood through the heart. Some labels may need to be used more than once. (Your teacher may select only certain labels for you to use.)

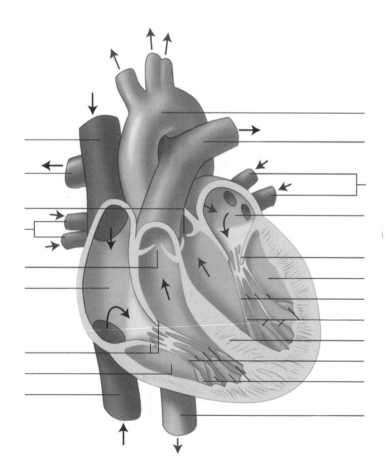

Internal anatomy of the heart and blood pathway through the heart.

EXERCISE 7.4

The Electrical Conduction System of the Heart

An intricate and continuous system of electrical conduction allows the heart to function properly. The following exercise will help you to understand this process more thoroughly by identifying the anatomical parts of the heart that facilitate it.

LABELS

- ❑ Atrioventricular (AV) node
- ❑ Bundle of HIS (AV bundle)
- ❑ Internodal pathways
- ❑ Purkinje fibres
- ❑ Right and left bundle branches
- ❑ Sinoatrial (SA) node

ELECTRICAL CONDUCTION COMPONENTS

Using the terms provided on the left, label the components involved in the conduction system of the heart in the diagram below. (Your teacher may select only certain labels for you to use.)

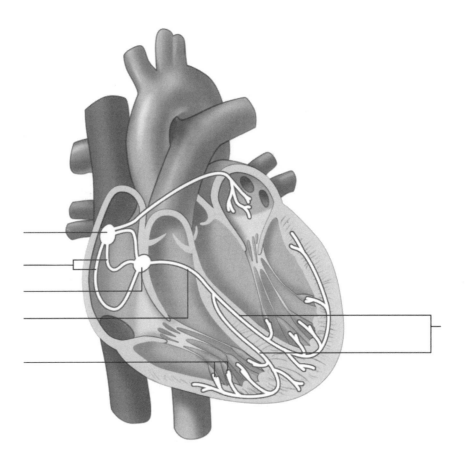

The electrical conduction system of the heart.

EXERCISE 7.5

The Anterior Structure of the Heart

The anterior view of the heart reveals many of its main components. This exercise will help you to become more familiar with many of the anatomical features of this complex organ.

LABELS

- Anterior interventricular branch of left coronary artery
- Aorta
- Branches of left pulmonary artery
- Branches of right pulmonary artery
- Great cardiac vein
- Inferior vena cava
- Left atrium
- Left pulmonary artery
- Left pulmonary veins
- Left ventricle
- Pulmonary trunk
- Right atrium
- Right coronary artery
- Right pulmonary veins
- Right ventricle
- Small cardiac vein
- Superior vena cava
- Thoracic aorta (descending)

THE HEART'S ANTERIOR VIEW

Using the terms provided on the left, label the diagram of the anterior view of the heart below. (Your teacher may select only certain labels for you to use.)

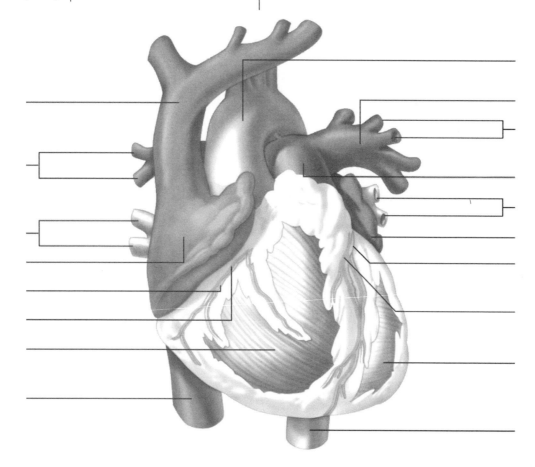

Anterior view of the coronary vessels, including other major heart structures.

EXERCISE 7.6

The Respiratory System

The human respiratory system is made up of many interconnected parts. The following exercise will help you to become familiar with several of its key components. Label the following diagram of the respiratory system, locating its main structures as indicated.

LABELS

- ❑ Alveolar sacs
- ❑ Conductive zone
- ❑ Epiglottis
- ❑ Larynx
- ❑ Mouth
- ❑ Nasal cavity
- ❑ Pharynx
- ❑ Pulmonary arteriole (carrying deoxygenated blood)
- ❑ Pulmonary venule (carrying oxygenated blood)
- ❑ Respiratory bronchiole
- ❑ Respiratory zone
- ❑ Right and left primary bronchi
- ❑ Secondary bronchi
- ❑ Smooth muscle
- ❑ Terminal bronchiole
- ❑ Tertiary bronchioles
- ❑ Trachea

Label the following diagram of the respiratory system, locating its main structures as indicated. (Your teacher may select only certain labels for you to use.)

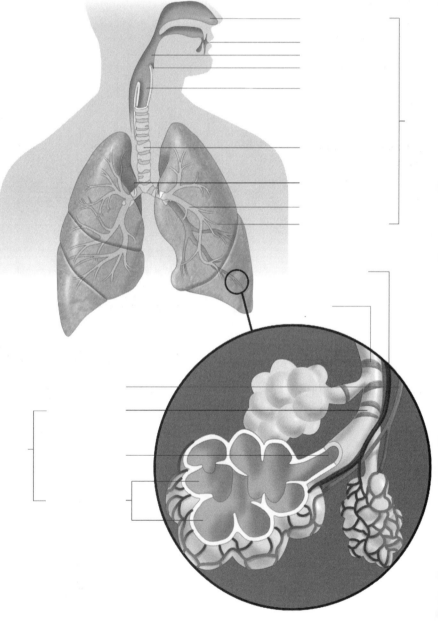

The main structures of the respiratory system.

EXERCISE 7.7

External and Internal Respiration

External respiration involves the exchange of O_2 and CO_2 in the lungs. Internal respiration refers to the exchange of gases at the tissue level, where O_2 is delivered and CO_2 is removed. Finally, in cellular respiration, the cells use O_2 to generate energy through the different metabolic pathways found in the mitochondria. This exercise will allow you to trace these pathways in detail to gain a better understanding of their direction and purpose.

LABELS

❏ Brain
❏ Cellular respiration
❏ CO_2
❏ External respiration
❏ Heart
❏ Internal respiration
❏ Lungs
❏ Mitochondria
❏ O_2
❏ Pulmonary arteries
❏ Pulmonary capillaries
❏ Pulmonary veins
❏ Systemic arteries
❏ Systemic capillaries
❏ Systemic veins
❏ Tissue cell

Label the illustration and colourize the blood flows (red–oxygenated; blue–deoxygenated). Some labels may need to be used more than once.

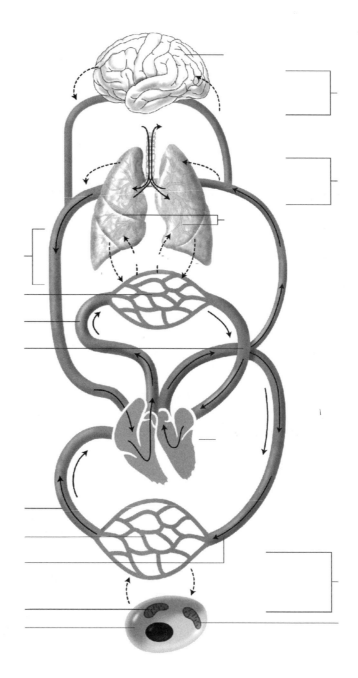

Flow diagram of external and internal respiration.

EXERCISE 7.8

Crossword on the Cardiovascular and Respiratory Systems

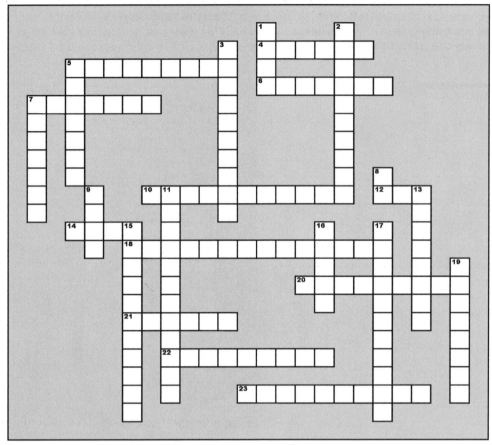

Across

4. Without this element, there would be no bodily tissue
5. Veins that carry oxygen-rich blood
6. Phase of contraction in the cardiac cycle
7. Shortness of breath
10. The combination of inspiration and expiration
12. This bundle is also known as the atrioventricular bundle
14. Acronym referring to recovery oxygen uptake
18. Process referring to the effects of chemical compounds on blood flow
20. This pathway is the site of movement for gases going from the lungs into the blood, from the blood to the tissue, and back
21. Acid that builds in the muscles during anaerobic exercise
22. The atrioventricular valve on the right side of the heart
23. The specialized muscle tissue of which the heart is composed

Down

1. An area of the brain stem important in the regulation of ventilation
2. A specialized protein found in erythrocytes
3. Controversial type of oxygen therapy
5. This type of recovery is attained through total rest
7. He has the highest VO_2max score on record
8. A measure of how acidic or basic blood is
9. Acronym for family of common respiratory diseases
11. The most abundant blood cells
13. As myocardium or cardiac muscle cells are said to act
15. Blood vessels of one-cell thickness
16. The upper chambers of the heart
17. Along with the apneustic, the pons contains this specialized respiratory centre
19. Tissue-level exchanges of gas comprise this form of respiration

8

Unit 1 Career Choices

Investigate a career in one of the fields covered in Unit 1. Ideally, you should interview someone working in the career for this assignment.

1. Career and description

_____
_____
_____
_____
_____
_____
_____
_____
_____
_____
_____

2. List at least two post-secondary institutions in Ontario and/or Canada that offer programs for this career.

_____
_____
_____
_____

3. Choose one of the above institutions and determine the required courses in the first year of study for this program.

_____
_____
_____
_____
_____
_____
_____
_____

4. What is the total length of the education needed to begin this career? Is an internship or apprenticeship required?

_____
_____
_____
_____

5. What is the average starting salary for this career? What is the top salary? On what do salary increases depend in this career?

_____
_____
_____
_____

6. What is the demand for individuals qualified for this occupation? If possible, provide some employment data to support the answer to this question.

_____
_____
_____
_____
_____
_____
_____

7. List occupational settings where a person with these qualifications could work.

_____
_____
_____
_____
_____

Unit 1 Crossword Challenge

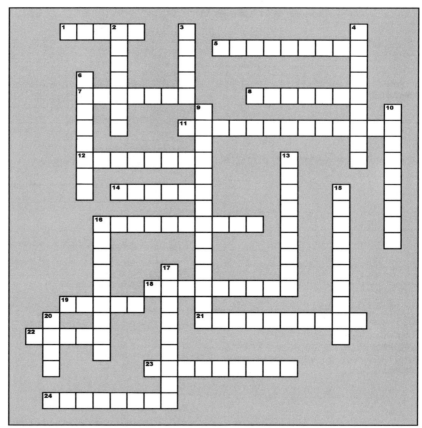

Across

1. Skeleton comprised mainly of the vertebral column, much of the skull, and the rib cage
5. The opposite of abduction
7. Type of joint bound tightly together with connective tissue, which allows no movement
8. Nervous system through which our awareness of the external environment operates
11. Term describing the movement of circling your arms in the air
12. Muscles that extend the limbs and increase the angle between two limbs
14. Muscles characterized by a high percentage of Type IIA and Type IIB fibres
16. Thread-like structures that run along the length of the muscle fibre
18. Tough bands of white, fibrous tissue that attach one or more bones together
19. Tendon organs that terminate where tendons join to muscle fibre
21. Also known as growth plates
22. Unit comprising the motor neuron, its axon, and the muscle fibre it stimulates
23. Large specialized muscle that separates the chest cavity from the abdominal cavity
24. Glucose is converted to this when it is stored within skeletal muscle and the liver

Down

2. System for resynthesizing ATP that takes place in the mitochondria
3. Cycle comprising a series of eight chemical reactions during which two ATP molecules are produced
4. Biological system that consists of glands
6. Nerves that carry information from sensory receptors to the central nervous system
9. Type of cartilage found mainly between the vertebrae of the spine
10. The point where the muscle attaches to the bone that is moved most
13. Shaft of the bone
15. A polysynaptic reflex that involves the withdrawal of a body part from a painful stimulus
16. Cavity found inside the shaft of the long bone
17. Movement of a gas, liquid, or solid from a region of high concentration to one of low concentration through random movement
20. Cycle in which lactic acid is converted to pyruvate for future conversion to glucose and glycogen

UNIT 2

HUMAN PERFORMANCE AND BIOMECHANICS

Notes

Lisa Faust and Karen Macneill, 1999. CP Photo/Frank Gunn.

10

Nutrition for Performance

LEARNING OBJECTIVES

The exercises in this section of the workbook will help to reinforce your knowledge of the following topics covered in the textbook:

- The importance of nutritional awareness for athletes and those who are physically active
- Macronutrients (proteins, carbohydrates, and fats) and miconutrients (vitamins, minerals, and water)
- Key vitamins and minerals
- Canada's Food Guide to Healthy Eating
- Dietary Reference Intakes
- Cholesterol and lipoproteins (including high-density and low-density lipoproteins)
- The "energy equation," and the process of counting calories
- How to develop a diet that matches performance requirements
- Basal and metabolic rates and how to calculate them
- How to estimate daily caloric needs
- The effect of exercise on fat loss and muscle gain
- The concept and calculation of Body Mass Index (BMI)
- Food labelling
- The controversy surrounding the "Zone Diet"
- The problem of obesity in Canada
- Weight management for athletes
- The role of nutrition in athletic performance, including competitive meals
- Dehydration and fluid replacement during athletic performance
- The concept of carbo-loading
- Heat cramps, heat stroke, and heat exhaustion

EXERCISE 10.1
Section Quiz

MULTIPLE-CHOICE QUESTIONS

Circle the letter beside the answer that you believe to be correct.

1. **Which one of the following statements best describes carbohydrates?**
   (a) they break down into amino acids
   (b) they contain 9 calories per gram
   (c) they contain 4 calories per gram
   (d) they have two subgroups called complete and incomplete

2. **Which one of the following best describes proteins?**
   (a) they contain 4 calories per gram
   (b) they can be grouped into complete and incomplete
   (c) there are 20 or so different types
   (d) all of the above

3. **Which one of the following statements can be said about fats?**
   (a) they contain 4 calories per gram
   (b) they can be grouped into complete and incomplete
   (c) they contain 9 calories per gram
   (d) none of the above

4. **Which one of the following vitamins are fat-soluble vitamins?**
   (a) C, D, and E
   (b) A, B, C, and K
   (c) B and C
   (d) A, D, E, and K

5. **Which of the following best describes iron?**
   (a) it aids in fat metabolism and can be found in most fruits and vegetables
   (b) most humans, especially women, get more than enough iron in their everyday diet
   (c) it helps build muscle, and can be found in all nutritional supplements
   (d) it helps carry oxygen and can be found in liver, tuna, and green leafy vegetables

6. **Basal metabolic rate can be simply defined as**
   (a) the rate at which your cardiovascular system uses energy
   (b) the rate at which all your muscle, taken together, use energy on a daily basis
   (c) the sum of all the essential energy needs for one's body to function
   (d) a rate of energy consumption that only applies to those who work out

SHORT-ANSWER QUESTIONS

Briefly answer the following questions in the space provided:

1. **Why are certain amino acids referred to as essential?**

2. **What are the three macronutrients?**

3. **What are the three micronutrients?**

4. **What percentage of our daily caloric intake should come from carbohydrates, fats, and proteins?**

5. **What is the difference between the seven key minerals and "trace" minerals?**

6. **What happens to arteries in the condition known as arteriosclerosis?**

7. **List some ways in which the body loses water.**

ESSAY QUESTIONS

On a separate sheet of paper, develop a 100-word response to the following questions:

1. **Name several food items that are an excellent source of iron and explain why iron is so important for female athletes.**

2. **What is the importance of hydration in training and competition? What beverage best fulfils the body's needs and why?**

3. **Explore the reasons for the rise in the levels of obesity in Canada. How can these best be addressed?**

EXERCISE 10.2

Terminology Review

DEFINING KEY TERMS

Briefly explain the meaning of the following key terms:

KEY TERM	DEFINITION
Macronutrients/micronutrients	
Complete/incomplete proteins	
Complex/simple carbohydrates	
Glycemic index	
Saturated/polyunsaturated fats	
Vitamins	
Minerals	
Water	
Canada's Food Guide to Healthy Eating	
Dietary Reference Intakes (DRIs)	
Cholesterol	
Atherosclerosis	
Energy equation	
Calorie	

Daily caloric need	
Metabolic rate (MR)	
Basal metabolic rate (BMR)	
Resting metabolic rate (RMR)	
Harris-Benedict equation	
Body Mass Index (BMI)	
Nutritional labelling	
Low-fat food diets	
Transfats	
Obesity/underweight	
Weight management	
Reflex dilation of skin	
Sweating reflex	
Dehydration	
Carbo-loading	
Heat cramps	
Heat exhaustion	
Heatstroke	

EXERCISE 10.3
Body Mass Index

Researchers and medical practitioners commonly use a measurement known as the Body Mass Index (BMI) to determine whether an individual is "balancing" the energy equation. In this exercise, you will become more familiar with this useful assessment tool.

BMI CALCULATION

Locate the point on the chart where your height and weight intersect to estimate your BMI and determine your BMI zone. Have five of your classmates, friends, or family do the same (write their initials on the chart).

Briefly answer the following question in the space provided:

What limitations does the BMI have?

_____

_____

_____

BMI Zones

- **Zone A** (< 20) – may be associated with health problems for some people;

- **Zone B** (20-25) – good weight for most people;

- **Zone C** (25-27) – may lead to health problems in some people;

- **Zone D** (>27) – increased risk of developing health problems.

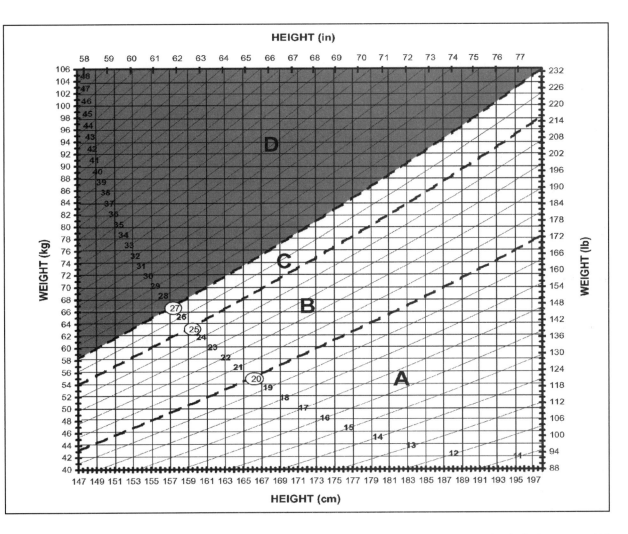

Health and Welfare Canada. (1988). Promoting healthy weights: A discussion paper. Minister of Supply and Services Canada: Ottawa, Ontario.

EXERCISE 10.4
Estimating Resting Metabolic Rate and Daily Caloric Need

Researchers use resting metabolic rate (RMR) to determine the essential energy requirements of an individual. From this RMR calculation, it is possible to compute an individual's daily caloric need. The following exercises will allow you to calculate your own RMR and daily caloric requirements.

RESTING METABOLIC RATE

A common way to compute resting metabolic rate is by using the Harris-Benedict equation. The figure resulting from this calculation is widely accepted as an estimate of RMR.

The Harris-Benedict formula adjusts for height, weight, and age by multiplying each by a factor (depending on whether you are male or female). To this figure is added a "constant" (again, varying by sex).

The Harris-Benedict equation is as follows:

RMR = constant + (__ x ht. in cm) + (__ x wt. in kg) – (__ x age)

In one of the tables below (depending on whether you are male or female), insert the numbers in the shaded areas so as to compute your RMR.

DAILY CALORIC NEED

It is easy to estimate your daily caloric need or the daily caloric intake necessary to maintain your current body weight. If you are not actively or otherwise put in little time at physical exercise, multiply RMR by 1.4. If you are active and engage in regular but moderate physical activity, multiply your RMR by a factor of 1.6. If you are highly active both at work and in physical activity, multiply RMR by a factor of 1.8.

RMR	Factor	Daily Caloric Need
	✗	**kcal/day**

Resting Metabolic Rate for Males					
Constant					66.5
Height	5	X	cm.	+	
Weight	13.7	X	kg.	+	
				Subtotal	
Age	6.8	X	yrs.	–	
				RESTING METABOLIC RATE =	

Resting Metabolic Rate for Females					
Constant					665
Height	1.9	X	cm.	+	
Weight	9.5	X	kg.	+	
				Subtotal	
Age	4.7	X	yrs.	–	
				RESTING METABOLIC RATE =	

EXERCISE 10.5
Making a Nutritional "Smoothie"

Eating wisely can further your goal of optimum nutrition for performance. This exercise will help you to become familiar with nutritional values in food and the importance of reading labels on prepared products.

LEARNING ABOUT NUTRITIONAL VALUES

In a small group (2-5 students), choose foods from the following list to make a blenderized "smoothie." If you prefer, and if the teacher approves the items beforehand, you may use different items.

(Tip: To make this activity easier, choose items that clearly show nutritional information on the container, or use ingredients for which such information is easily found.)

Complete the table below as well as the food label on the next page with the nutritional information for your creation. Give the concoction a name and develop a short promotional description that focuses on explaining the nutritional value of your new creation. If your teacher is willing, you might carry out this exercise in class, followed by a taste challenge.

Use the following website to acquire your nutritional food values:

http://www.nal.usda.gov/fnic/foodcomp

Ingredient	Approx. Grams Used	Carbo-hydrate per Gram	Fat per Gram	Protein per gram	Total Energy	Choles-terol	Sodium	Vitamin A	Vitamin C	Calcium	Iron	Fibre
Ice cream/ frozen yoghurt												
Banana												
Apple												
Chocolate syrup												
Pineapple juice												
Yoghurt												
Kiwi												
Strawberry												
Cantaloupe												
Peach												
Watermelon												
Totals												

Descriptive Label for Your Food Creation

_____

_____
_____
_____
_____

Nutrition Facts

Per _____mL (_____g)

Amount	% Daily Value

Calories _____

Fat _____g	_____%
Saturated _____g	
+ Trans _____g	_____%
Cholesterol _____mg	
Sodium _____mg	_____%
Carbohydrate _____g	_____%
Fibre _____g	_____%
Sugars _____g	
Protein _____g	

Vitamin A _____%	Vitamin C _____%
Calcium _____%	Iron _____%

EXERCISE 10.6
Nutrition and Physical Activity

If you are an active person, it is necessary to compare your daily energy requirements with your daily energy expenditure. This exercise will allow you to explore the relationship between nutrition and physical activity by comparing these two factors and determining if this relationship is a balanced one.

BALANCING THE ENERGY EQUATION

Insert your **resting metabolic rate** score and then calculate your **daily caloric need** using a factor based on your level of activity (see Exercise 10.4).

Record your food intake for a three-day period on the chart provided. (Summarize if necessary.)

On this page, write in your estimated average daily energy intake from food after three days and compare this with the daily caloric need calculation just above it. Of course, these figures will not be the same.

If the difference is great, you might want to speculate as to why there is such a great difference – perhaps you are more active than you think (or perhaps not as active).

Your three-day food values can be acquired from http://www.nal.usda.gov/fnic/foodcomp or entered using the N.A.T. (Nutritional Analysis Tool) at http://www.nat.uiuc.edu

Resting Metabolic Rate	
Daily Caloric Intake Estimate	
Estimated daily energy intake from food after 3 days *(taken from bottom of page 117)*	

	APPROX. GRAMS USED	CARBO-HYDRATE PER GRAM	FAT PER GRAM	PROTEIN PER GRAM	TOTAL ENERGY	VITAMIN A	VITAMIN C	CALCIUM	IRON

Day 1 Food Intake

	APPROX. GRAMS USED	CARBO-HYDRATE PER GRAM	FAT PER GRAM	PROTEIN PER GRAM	TOTAL ENERGY	VITAMIN A	VITAMIN C	CALCIUM	IRON
DAY 1 TOTALS									

Day 2 Food Intake

DAY 2 TOTALS									

	APPROX. GRAMS USED	CARBO-HYDRATE PER GRAM	FAT PER GRAM	PROTEIN PER GRAM	TOTAL ENERGY	VITAMIN A	VITAMIN C	CALCIUM	IRON

Day 3 Food Intake

DAY 3 TOTALS									

| **OVERALL TOTALS** | | | | | | | | | |

EXERCISE 10.7
Nutrient Sources

The previous exercise allowed you to explore the relationship between your daily exercise regimen and your daily nutritional requirements. The following activity will allow you to develop a deeper understanding of exactly how the human body can obtain key nutrients and vitamins from the food we eat.

SUMMARY TABLE

Fill in the missing information in the summary tables below.

MACRONUTRIENT	CALORIES PER GRAM	MAJOR SUBDIVISIONS
Carbohydrates		
Protein		
Fat		

VITAMIN	MAIN FOOD SOURCES
A	
B$_1$	
B$_2$	
B$_3$	
B$_6$	
B$_{12}$	
C	
D	
E	
K	
Iron	
Calcium	
Phosphorous	

11

Performance-Enhancing Substances and Techniques

LEARNING OBJECTIVES

The exercises in this section of the workbook will help to reinforce your knowledge of the following topics covered in the textbook:

- The three basic forms of performance-enhancing substances, or ergogenic aids (nutritional, pharmacological, and physiological aids)
- The basic subgroups of nutritional aids (vitamins and minerals; proteins and amino acid supplements; carnitine; creatine; and caffeine)
- The basic subgroups of pharmacological aids (pain-masking drugs, anabolic steroids, prohormones, human growth hormone, and erythropoietin)
- The role of the World Anti-Doping Agency in fighting drug use in sport
- The role of the Canadian Centre for Ethics in Sport in opposing illegal dug use and other unethical sport practices
- The International Olympic Committee's list of banned pharmacological substances
- The drug policies of various professional sports
- The use of physiological aids such as blood doping and drug masking
- The Dubin Inquiry and its impact on Canadian sport
- Drug testing practices in sport
- The ethical implications of drug use in sport

EXERCISE 11.1
Section Quiz

MULTIPLE-CHOICE QUESTIONS

Circle the letter beside the answer that you believe to be correct.

1. The artificial development of muscle tissue is promoted by the use of
    (a) anabolic steroids
    (b) erythropoietin
    (c) blood doping
    (d) caffeine

2. Athletes who compete in endurance sports may try to enhance their performance by taking
    (a) anabolic steroids
    (b) erythropoietin
    (c) beta-blockers
    (d) human growth hormone

3. Which of the following ergogenic techniques does not involve ingesting a substance?
    (a) drug masking
    (b) creatine
    (c) blood doping
    (d) human growth hormone

4. Which of the following performance-enhancing substances is difficult to detect?
    (a) human growth hormone
    (b) synthetic testosterone
    (c) erythropoietin
    (d) all of the above

5. Which of the following substances have athletes used to promote fat loss?
    (a) carnitine
    (b) protein supplements
    (c) creatine
    (d) caffeine

6. Which of the following ergogenic aids is used to enhance aerobic athletic performance?
    (a) blood doping
    (b) creatine
    (c) erythropoietin
    (d) a and c

7. The Canadian Centre for Ethics in Sport is concerned with
    (a) an ethical clean up of the sporting world
    (b) promoting fair play through educational outlets
    (c) opposing the use of drugs in sport
    (d) all of the above

SHORT-ANSWER QUESTIONS

Briefly answer the following questions in the space provided:

1. What must an Olympic competitor do if he or she wishes to use medicines that contain banned substances?

2. What method is used to test for banned substances?

3. What do beta blockers do?

4. Which common stimulant has been banned by the International Olympic Committee? Why?

5. What are the general negative side effects of ingesting extra human growth hormone?

6. Name four pain-masking agents used by athletes.

7. Which governing body banned Ben Johnson for life from competing in track and field?

8. What did the Dubin Inquiry seek to ascertain?

9. What are the components of successful drug testing?

ESSAY QUESTIONS

On a separate sheet of paper, develop a 100-word response to the following questions:

1. Describe one ergogenic aid from each classification (nutritional, pharmacological, physiological). In which sports would athletes benefit from the use of these aids?

2. Describe the drug policies of three of the five major-league sports.

3. Summarize Canada's drug scandal at the 1988 Seoul Olympics and explain the worldwide significance of this event.

EXERCISE 11.2
Terminology Review

DEFINING KEY TERMS

Briefly explain the meaning of the following key terms:

KEY TERM	DEFINITION
Nutritional supplements	
Protein and amino acid supplements	
Carnitine	
Creatine	
Caffeine	
Deceptive advertising	
Doping	
Pain-masking agents	
World Anti-Doping Agency	

Anabolic steroids	
Prohormones	
Human growth hormone (HGH)	
Canadian Centre for Ethics in Sport (CCES)	
Erythropoietin (EPO)	
Restricted pharmacological substances	
Drug policies	
Blood doping	
Drug masking	
Dubin Inquiry	
Drug testing	

EXERCISE 11.3

The Effects of Performance-Enhancing Drugs and Techniques

When the rewards of winning take precedence over the principle of fair play, athletes may resort to banned drugs and techniques to improve their performance. This exercise will help you gain familiarity with the immediate enhancing effects of several of these drugs and techniques, as well as their associated health risks.

PERFORMANCE-ENHANCERS AND THEIR EFFECTS

Research the listed substances and techniques, and complete the table below.

TYPE	USE AND EFFECTS	HEALTH RISKS
Anabolic agents		
Diuretics		
Narcotics		
Stimulants		
Hormones		
Blood doping		
Beta-blockers		

EXERCISE 11.4

The Canadian Centre for Ethics in Sport — Research Exercise

The CCES is engaged in a variety of initiatives with leading sport organizations, public authorities, and the private sector in promoting ethical conduct. This exercise will introduce you to the role played by CCES and the goals of these initiatives.

THE CCES AND ITS ACTIVITIES

Research the following initiatives on the CCES website (www.cces.ca) and fill in the table below.

CCES INITIATIVE	GOALS
Canadian Strategy for Ethical Conduct in Sport	
Alternative Dispute Resolution Board	
The Spirit of Sport Foundation	
National Sport Ethics Forum	
Champion for Life	
Research	

12

Technological Influences on Human Performance

LEARNING OBJECTIVES

The exercises in this section of the workbook will help to reinforce your knowledge of the following topics covered in the textbook:

- The impact that various scientific practices have had on sport performance
- The field of ergonomics and its role in sport
- How technology has improved the design and construction of personal protective equipment in a number of sports
- How technology has improved the design and construction of sports equipment such as clothing, playing surfaces, and so on
- The impact of advances in computer technology on sport

EXERCISE 12.1
Section Quiz

MULTIPLE-CHOICE QUESTIONS

Circle the letter beside the answer that you believe to be correct.

1. **Helmets can reduce the energy absorbed by the skull in a cycling mishap (when riding at a common cycling speed of 15 km per hour) by**
   (a) 15 percent
   (b) 25 percent
   (c) 90 percent
   (d) 50 percent

2. **Athletes can use equipment that manufacturers claim will compress muscles, thereby limiting tissue vibration, in**
   (a) track and field
   (b) swimming
   (c) race car driving
   (d) a and b

3. **The Polara golf ball was banned by the U.S. Golf Association because**
   (a) of its cellular construction
   (b) it reduced the skills necessary to play golf
   (c) of its asymmetrical shape
   (d) it increased the likelihood of hooks and slices

4. **Ten Olympic records were broken in the speed skating competition at the Nagano Winter Olympics in 1998 because of**
   (a) innovative bodysuits
   (b) an improved ice surface
   (c) clap skates
   (d) computerized timing equipment

5. **The most critical material invention in sportswear was that of**
   (a) Lycra
   (b) elastic
   (c) cotton
   (d) plastic

6. **In recent years, the re-design of football equipment has been crucial because**
   (a) rule changes have allowed players to wear less protection
   (b) rule changes have allowed greater physical contact
   (c) players have demanded less expensive equipment
   (d) heat-related injuries have become increasingly common

7. **As bicycles have become more efficient, which traditional element have designers eliminated?**
   (a) gear shifters
   (b) crossbars
   (c) hand brakes
   (d) rubberized tires

SHORT-ANSWER QUESTIONS

Briefly answer the following questions in the space provided:

1. Describe the role of an ergonomist in sport.

2. Describe the evolution of fabrics in sportswear.

3. What are the three main evolutionary changes in track events?

4. Describe how the clap skate has enhanced performance in speed skating.

5. Outline the controversy over the introduction of the new soccer ball, Fevernova, at the 2002 World Cup soccer.

6. What are the drawbacks to artificial turf?

7. Describe an example of an equipment design innovation that challenged the integrity of the sport when it was introduced.

8. Which sports have already used virtual reality simulators to help their athletes train?

ESSAY QUESTIONS

On a separate sheet of paper, develop a 100-word response to the following questions:

1. Discuss the dilemma for sports organizations in their relationship with technology.

2. Explain how the evolution of equipment has enhanced human performance with respect to three sports.

3. Examine how coaching has been affected by the revolutionary changes in the application of computer technology to sport.

EXERCISE 12.2
Terminology Review

DEFINING KEY TERMS

Briefly explain the meaning of the following key terms:

KEY TERM	DEFINITION
Ergonomics	
Repetitive stress injury	
Personal protective equipment	
Equipment revolution	
Wicking properties	
Clap skate	
Full-body swimsuits	
Lifting shirt	
Artificial turf	
Motion analysis	
Virtual reality technologies	

EXERCISE 12.3

The Equipment Revolution

The creation of new sports equipment is dramatically changing athletic performance, including the cost of participating, the skills necessary to succeed in a particular sport, and the injuries associated with that sport. This exercise will allow you to research the impact of the revolution in engineering and materials design on particular sports.

CHANGES IN SPORT EQUIPMENT

Research the following pieces of sports equipment. For each, complete the chart, noting the equipment's "evolution" and the criticism or drawbacks that have accompanied major changes. Choose three pieces of equipment from other sports and fill in the chart. The first entry has been completed to assist you.

	EQUIPMENT CHANGES	CRITICISM/DRAWBACKS
Hockey stick	Early North American wood sticks; more advanced wood/fibreglass design; graphite sticks	Hockey "purists" say graphite offers less control; too much curve in blade leads to poor shooting technique
Tennis racquet		
Soccer ball		
Swimsuits		
Athletic shoes		
Track surfaces		
Skates		
Bicycle		

EXERCISE 12.4

Sport Organizations and Technology

Sports organizations have often banned the use of technologically improved equipment, arguing that it erodes the particular skills and traditions of their sport. This exercise will introduce you to the particular concerns of sports organizations and the larger question of whether improved athletic performance is due to higher skill levels or the engineering of better sports equipment.

CONTROVERSIAL EQUIPMENT INNOVATIONS

(A) Research the following sports equipment and fill in the chart below. Choose another example of controversial sport equipment and complete the chart.

EQUIPMENT	SPORT	REASON FOR CONTROVERSY
Polara golf ball		
Full-body swimsuits		
Clap skates		
Inzer lifting shirt		

(B) Once you have completed the chart above, answer the following questions:

To what extent do you believe that improved athletic performance is due to the improved engineering and materials now used in sports equipment? To what extent is it due to higher skill levels? Give examples to support your answers.

EXERCISE 12.5

Crossword on Technological Influences on Human Performance

Across

1. This part of the clap skate is spring-loaded
3. "Reality" that uses models to create totally new views of real events
6. Dynamic that pulls a cyclist backward
9. Stress injury affecting tendons, nerves, muscles, and other soft body tissue
11. Sport that introduced controversial Fevernova ball
13. Turf reputed to cause injuries to ligaments, joints, and tendons
14. What gasoline does at temperatures reaching 1,149°C
17. Material formerly used to make baseball helmets
21. Synthetic material used in modern tennis racquets
22. Property of athletic clothing describing their ability to draw moisture away from the skin
23. Item used to clock track events before the introduction of digital timing
24. Fibre used to construct the structural parts of a race car
25. Entire athletic garments are now made from this elasticized material
26. Body part emulated by the seams of the Fastskin swimsuit

Down

2. Designer of controversial shirt for weightlifters
4. This science is sometimes called "human-factors engineering"
5. Mandatory protective gear in the NHL
7. Advances in materials can now protect football players from this potentially fatal condition
8. The reduction of friction by lessening wind contact
10. Users can interact realistically with this technologically created reality
12. Ergonomists use this term to describe individual differences
15. Type of base that prevents common foot and leg injuries for softball players
16. Personal equipment that measures hip undulations or strides and thereby distance travelled
18. Athletes now benefit from precision analysis of this
19. What athletic socks are now designed to eliminate
20. The human touch of this key sports figure is being challenged by technology

13

Training Principles and Methods

LEARNING OBJECTIVES

The exercises in this section of the workbook will help to reinforce your knowledge of the following topics covered in the textbook:

- Definition of athletic training and its parameters
- The F.I.T.T. principle (Frequency, Intensity, Time, and Type) of developing a training program
- The role of cardiorespiratory fitness measurement in designing training schedules
- The role of the three energy systems in training
- The six Principles of training (Overload, Progression, Specificity, Individual Difference, Reversibility, and Diminishing Returns), and their integration into an individual training regimen
- The six methods of training (periodization, concurrent, interval, Fartlek, resistance, and plyometrics)
- The general adaptation syndrome (GAS), and its role in athletic training
- Environmental factors and their impact on training
- Other important factors that can have an effect on training, such as rest, recovery, avoiding injury, maintaining interest, and avoiding burnout and/or overtraining

EXERCISE 13.1
Section Quiz

MULTIPLE-CHOICE QUESTIONS

Circle the letter beside the answer that you believe to be correct.

1. **The acronym F.I.T.T.**
   (a) was coined by Canadian Dr. David M. Chisholm
   (b) captures the four basic building blocks of an exercise plan
   (c) stands for frequency, intensity, type, and time of training
   (d) all of the above

2. **The formula whereby one's age is subtracted from 220 is**
   (a) the most accurate way of predicting maximal heart rate
   (b) recommended only for elite athletes
   (c) an accurate assessment of heart rate
   (d) an estimation of maximal heart rate

3. **The baseline values for training frequency within the F.I.T.T. principle are**
   (a) 1-2 times per week
   (b) 3-5 times per week
   (c) 3-7 times per week
   (d) 1-5 times per week

4. **Which type of activity utilizes the anaerobic system?**
   (a) sprints
   (b) high speed, explosive movements
   (c) long-distance running
   (d) both a and b

5. **What is the recommended number of sets for an expert athlete seeking to attain hypertrophy as outlined by the ACSM?**
   (a) greater or equal to five
   (b) greater or equal to three
   (c) greater or equal to one
   (d) greater or equal to four

6. **Which principle states that loads must be increased in order for adaptation to occur?**
   (a) Individual Differences
   (b) Overload
   (c) Specificity
   (d) S.A.I.D

7. **Which type of training involves multiple system training (sometimes called "cross training")?**
   (a) concurrent
   (b) Fartlek
   (c) interval
   (d) plyometric

SHORT-ANSWER QUESTIONS

Briefly answer the following questions in the space provided:

1. **What are some of the potential benefits and drawbacks of Fartlek training?**

2. **What is PNF stretching? How does it work?**

3. **What is involved in interval training?**

4. **How could the Overload Principle be implemented into an existing training program?**

5. **Outline the parameters of the F.I.T.T. Principle.**

6. **Define the term "repetition maximum."**

7. **Name three long-term steady exercises for which the aerobic system supplies the energy.**

8. **Name three variables that should be taken into account when considering a weight-training program.**

ESSAY QUESTIONS

On a separate sheet of paper, develop a 100-word response to the following questions:

1. **Using the HRR and MHR method, calculate a THR of 75 percent for a sixteen-year-old individual who has a resting heart rate of 80 beats per minute. State why one method is more accurate than the other.**

2. **Outline how the concept of periodization works.**

3. **The General Adaptation Syndrome (GAS) was devised in the mid-1950s by stress researcher Hans Seyle. Explain the three stages that our body goes through in response to stress according to this theory.**

EXERCISE 13.2
Terminology Review

DEFINING KEY TERMS

Briefly explain the meaning of the following key terms:

KEY TERM	DEFINITION
Target heart rate (THR)	
Maximal heart rate (MHR)	
Heart rate reserve (HRR)	
Borg Scale of Perceived Exertion	
F.I.T.T. Principle	
One repetition maximum (1RM)	
Repetition maximum (RM)	
Principle of Overload	
Principle of Progression	
Specificity Principle (the S.A.I.D. Principle)	
Principle of Individual Differences	

Principle of Reversibility	
Principle of Diminishing Returns	
Periodization	
The General Adaptation Syndrome (GAS)	
Concurrent training	
Interval training	
Fartlek training	
Resistance training	
Plyometrics training	
Cold stress and heat stress	
Thermoregulation	
Heat exchange	
Acclimatization	
Proprioceptive neuromuscular facilitation	
Burnout and overtraining	

EXERCISE 13.3
Training Principles and Methods Research

People often adopt training schedules published in books and magazines or on the Internet in an attempt to further their athletic goals. In this exercise, you will assess the effectiveness of some of these recommended methods.

TRAINING SCHEDULE EVALUATION

From the library, a local bookstore, or the Internet, select three different magazine articles that deal with some aspect of athletic or physical training. Avoid articles dealing with general "health benefits" – your aim is to select articles that deal with a specific aspect of training to improve performance in some sport or activity.

All should focus on the same topic, i.e., weight training, stretching, proper nutrition strategies, interval training for recreational walkers, training to improve your time in a 10-km running race, and so on. You should, however, attempt to select three that are aimed at varying levels of ability: one article for beginners, one for those at an intermediate and/or recreational level, and one for those who are advanced participants in the sport or activity.

Compare and contrast the three articles using the chart below. A fictional sample article entry has been included to assist you.

CRITERIA	SAMPLE ARTICLE	ARTICLE 1	ARTICLE 2	ARTICLE 3
Name of magazine	Recreational Walker's World Magazine			
Article title	Interval training: "Just one workout a week can make a big difference!"			
Author / Qualifications	Dr. Peter Walker, Ph.D., exercise physiologist, U. of Alberta			
Overall claim	Incorporating one interval workout a week can help the recreational walker improve fitness and can add enjoyment to his or her exercise schedule.			
Body focus (i.e., energy system, muscle group, etc.)	Primary: cardiovascular system Secondary: leg muscle strength/ endurance			

CRITERIA	SAMPLE ARTICLE	ARTICLE 1	ARTICLE 2	ARTICLE 3
Steps to success/program outline	Walkers begin by adding faster "bursts" of 3-5 minutes into ordinarily steady-state walking; rest intervals begin at 2-4 minutes and are then decreased. Pulse rate monitoring also recommended.			
Duration of program	12-week cycle is recommended, although author also offers 3- and 6-week cycle schedules.			
Advantages of the strategies outlined	Incorporating intervals may break up monotony of constant steady walking for many. Faster walking interspersed with rest intervals will improve cardiovascular capacity according to theory of interval training.			
Problems with the strategies outlined	Program may be too "intense" for many recreational walkers. Extra fatigue incurred during these workouts may decrease enjoyment for many.			
General comments	Very well organized; author seems to understand aims of average recreational walker. Emphasis on enjoyment a big plus. Many walkers may not be aware of alternative training modes like this.			
Your overall evaluation of the article's effectiveness (Scale 1-10)	8.5			

EXERCISE 13.4

The Effect of Environmental Factors on Training and Performance

A number of environmental factors can have a significant impact on physical training, including hot or cold air temperatures, altitude, and humidity. In this exercise, you will have the opportunity to examine "real life" instances in which these factors significantly affected performance.

ENVIRONMENTAL FACTORS AND TRAINING

Using the Internet, newspapers, magazines, books, or video as the basis of your research, fill in the chart below with historical or current examples of how the environmental factors indicated have had an impact on training and/or competition. (A sample entry has been included to assist you.)

ENVIRONMENTAL FACTOR	EFFECTS ON THE BODY AND TRAINING
High Altitude	At the track and field competition in the1968 Olympic Games in Mexico City, every long-distance event was won in a time significantly slower than the world record. Athletes born and raised at high altitudes dominated; those from sea-level areas attempted to train at altitude to prepare but almost none of their efforts were successful. Athletes in sprints, however, recorded many excellent times due to the "thinner" air.
Cold Climates	
Hot Climates (with high humidity)	
Air Quality	

EXERCISE 13.5

Crossword on Training Principles and Methods

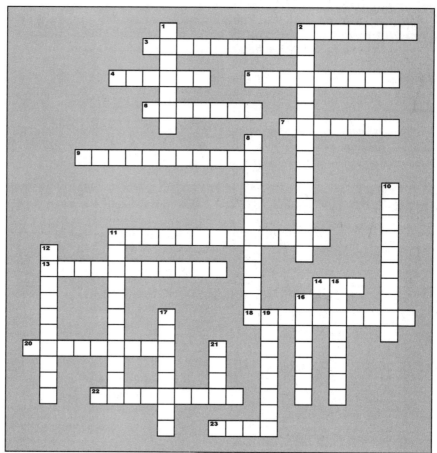

Across

2. Muscle condition resulting from inactivity
3. Type of training that involves box jumping
4. Cool-down sessions can reduce the build-up of this acid
5. Type of stretching that involves bouncing
6. Swedish word for "speed play" training
7. Interval training pioneer
9. Training principle that states that performance outcomes must match training exercises
11. Term used to describe the breaking down of training into time-specific segments
13. Process in which sweat is vaporized from the skin into the environment
14. The maximal amount of weight an individual can lift for one repetition
18. Most athletes follow a routine of this type of exercise to increase muscle flexibility
20. The first person to break the 4-minute mile
22. What the "I" in F.I.T.T. represents
23. Person who devised the scale of perceived exertion

Down

1. Term for state in which training and/or competition performance stops improving
2. Process whereby the body adjusts to high altitude
8. Group of neurons located at the base of the brain that maintain the body's temperature
10. Type of training that combines resistance and endurance training
11. Performing your workouts faster each week is an example of this training principle
12. A method of training that involves using weight
15. Sleep and rest are essential to this element of any training regimen
16. Long-distance running, cycling, and swimming train this energy system
17. Another name for the heart rate reserve method
19. A "vehicle" used to make the body more efficient
21. This type of exchange is achieved by radiation, conduction, and evaporation

14
Personal Fitness and Training

LEARNING OBJECTIVES

The exercises in this section of the workbook will help to reinforce your knowledge of the following topics covered in the textbook:

- Ways of determining a person's goals and level of commitment before embarking on training
- How to develop measurable objectives for a training program
- Methods of assessing a person's lifestyle prior to beginning training
- Tools for assessing personal fitness, including the CPAFLA protocol
- Ways of testing for specific areas of fitness, including cardiovascular fitness, body composition, muscular strength and endurance, and flexibility
- Basic guidelines for developing an exercise program, for the improvement of both aerobic and anaerobic capacity
- The design of specialized exercise plans, including those aimed at improving cardiovascular conditioning, managing body weight, enhancing muscle flexibility, and promoting resistance training methods.
- How to develop specialized fitness plans for individuals with varying needs and at varying levels of fitness
- Pertinent safety issues in designing fitness programs

EXERCISE 14.1
Section Quiz

MULTIPLE-CHOICE QUESTIONS

Circle the letter beside the answer that you believe to be correct.

1. **Which of the following is an example of a fitness objective?**
   (a) developing a more active lifestyle
   (b) recovering from an injury
   (c) improving athletic performance
   (d) all of the above

2. **Which of the following fitness appraisals is a test for muscular endurance?**
   (a) Body Mass Index
   (b) grip strength
   (c) push-ups
   (d) all of the above

3. **Circuit training is effective if you are seeking to**
   (a) develop cardiorespiratory fitness and lay the foundation for sport-specific aerobic activity
   (b) develop cardiovascular fitness and reduce the incidence of sport-specific injuries
   (c) improve your heart rate reserve percentage
   (d) increase the time in which you can endure anaerobic activity

4. **Anaerobic exercise should include**
   (a) low levels of resistance training
   (b) speed and agility
   (c) strength and power development
   (d) both b and c

5. **Flexibility is important in exercise because it**
   (a) aids in increasing muscle hypertrophy
   (b) plays a major role in the maintenance of muscle balance
   (c) helps you to strengthen your muscles and reduce the risk of injury
   (d) increases the range of motion in your muscles

6. **If aerobic training is a primary objective, the days between workouts should be no more than**
   (a) one
   (b) two
   (c) three
   (d) four

7. **The benefits of stretching include**
   (a) increasing the ROM of joints
   (b) helping to nourish the joint's connective tissue
   (c) enhancing muscle length
   (d) all of the above

8. **Which of the following is the best preventative method of avoiding overtraining?**
   (a) adequate short term recovery
   (b) proper variation
   (c) careful monitoring
   (d) all of the above

SHORT-ANSWER QUESTIONS

Briefly answer the following questions in the space provided:

1. **Outline the three stages involved in developing a sound fitness training program.**

2. **What are three possible objectives of an individual's exercise program?**

3. **What are the elements of a healthy lifestyle?**

4. **Describe various testing methods to assess cardiovascular endurance.**

5. **Outline CPAFLA's approach to healthy body composition testing.**

6. **In designing an exercise program, what are the two main criteria for selecting appropriate exercises?**

7. **What are the three steps to consider when using interval training in an exercise program?**

8. **Why is a cooling-down period very important in an anaerobic program?**

ESSAY QUESTIONS

On a separate sheet of paper, develop a 100-word response to the following questions:

1. **Design a personal anaerobic fitness program to suit an athlete in the sport of your choice.**

2. **Summarize the components of fitness that are emphasized in the Canadian Activity, Fitness and Lifestyle Approach and describe how they are tested.**

3. **The best solution to losing excess fat is to have an exercise program that combines aerobic exercise and light resistance training. Design a program for an individual who has cleared the PAR-Q questionnaire that would facilitate a reasonable loss of fat over a period of 8 weeks.**

EXERCISE 14.2
Terminology Review

DEFINING KEY TERMS

Briefly explain the meaning of the following key terms:

KEY TERM	DEFINITION
Fitness objectives	
Motivational readiness	
FANTASTIC Lifestyle Checklist	
Performance-related fitness	
Health-related fitness	
The Canadian Physical Activity, Fitness and Lifestyle Appraisal (CPAFLA)	
Cardiovascular endurance	
Body composition	
Muscular strength	
Muscular endurance	
Flexibility	
Léger "Beep Test"	

EXERCISE 14.3

Crossword on Personal Fitness and Training

Across

2. High levels of this acid are produced during anaerobic training
4. The flexibility of this body part can be measured by the Trunk Forward Flexion Test
9. Aspect of exercises that affects fatigue, safety, and results
10. The ability of a joint to move freely through its full range of motion
11. Type of training that achieves the greatest amount of work with the least fatigue
12. A solid aerobic base should be established prior to this type of training
14. Desires to meet needs in specific ways
17. Endurance of this type is generally regarded as the best indicator of overall health
19. Test for aerobic fitness developed by Dr. Luc Léger
20. The mCAFT is one example of this type of test
22. The ability of a muscle to perform repeated or sustained contractions over a period of time
23. Maximal uptake of this element is most precisely determined through direct gas analysis in a laboratory

Down

1. A type of anthropometric measurement
3. Tests such as the T-test measure this physical quality
5. Acronym for the current version of the 1979 Canadian Standardized Test of Fitness
6. Readiness for physical fitness training determined by the Stages of Change Questionnaire
7. Trying to improve this is key for those striving to succeed in sport or work
8. Muscular quality defined as the maximum tension or force a muscle can exert in a single contraction
13. These must be clear before designing a fitness program
15. The most important but taxing part of an aerobic program
16. Diseases due to these kinds of choices are the major causes of disability and death
18. The resistance provided by free weights and stack weights
19. Key values assessed for selected components of fitness against which progress can be measured
20. Tissue that stores fat
21. A screening device administered prior to a fitness assessment

EXERCISE 14.4

Personal Fitness Assessment and Exercise Program Design

An important aspect of practising a healthy active lifestyle involves assessing and evaluating your own fitness level and adjusting your lifestyle to attain certain goals. This next series of activities will allow you to assess your fitness level and design an appropriate fitness program.

1. PERSONAL FITNESS ASSESSMENT EXERCISE

First, complete the Health and Lifestyle Appraisal on the following page (**Fantastic Lifestyle Checklist**) to help determine which factors affect your overall health and well-being. Reflect on any habits or attitudes that you may wish to change:

_____

_____

_____

_____

_____

2. PAR-Q (PHYSICAL ACTIVITY, FITNESS AND LIFESTYLE APPRAISAL)

Next, fill out the **Par-Q (Physical Activity, Fitness and Lifestyle Appraisal)** to address any health related problems that should be considered. You will find the Par-Q Questionnaire on page 145 of this workbook.

3. HEALTH-RELATED FITNESS ASSESSMENT

The third stage is to complete a series of health-related fitness assessments. These will involve fitness testing procedures taken from the Canadian Physical Activity, Fitness and Lifestyle Appraisal (CPAFLA) guide, as well as some additional tests. The tests are grouped in three categories: (a) Body Composition Assessment; (b) Cardiovascular Assessment; (c) Musculoskeletal Fitness Assessment. These three sets of tests are presented on the following pages.

During the fitness tests, record your results in the summary chart provided on the page following the PAR-Q Questionnaire. For your results in each of the tests, refer to the scales reproduced in various appendices at the end of this workbook.

4. INTERPRET YOUR RESULTS

The fourth stage is to interpret your results by answering the following questions:

- In which test did you achieve your best results?

_____

- In which test did your results prove to be poor?

_____

- Why do you think this was so?

_____

_____

- Did your results equal your expectations of what you thought you were capable of?

_____

- Your reactions as to how you place on the "health benefit zones."

_____

- With reference to specific components of fitness, how could you improve your overall results?

_____

5. DESIGN AN EXERCISE PROGRAM TO MEET YOUR PERSONAL NEEDS

Once you have completed your fitness appraisal and assessed your results, you are ready to design an exercise program to meet your personal needs. Apply the F.I.T.T. principle and other training principles (found in Section 13 of your textbook) when designing your sixteen-week aerobic/anaerobic resistance training program. Retest after the sixteen weeks to determine any improvements in your overall fitness. Use Table 14.10 on page 222 of the textbook as a template for your program design.

FANTASTIC LIFESTYLE CHECKLIST

Instructions: Unless otherwise specified, place an "X" beside the box that best describes your behaviour or situation in the past month.

Family Friends	I have someone to talk to about things that are important to me	Almost never		Seldom		Some of the time		Fairly often		Almost always	
	I give and receive affection	Almost never		Seldom		Some of the time		Fairly often		Almost always	
Activity	I am vigorously active for at least 30 minutes per day (e.g., running, cycling, etc.)	Less than once a week		1-2 times/ week		3 times/ week		4 times/ week		5 or more times/ week	
	I am moderately active (e.g., gardening, climbing stairs, walking, housework)	Less than once a week		1-2 times/ week		3 times/ week		4 times/ week		5 or more times/ week	
Nutrition	I eat a balanced diet	Almost never		Seldom		Some of the time		Fairly often		Almost always	
	I often eat excess: 10 sugar, or 12 salt or 16 animal fats or 14 junk foods	4 of these		3 of these		2 of these		1 of these		None of these	
	I am within ____ kg of my healthy weight	Not within 8 kg (20 lbs.)		8 kg (20 lbs.)		6 kg (15 lbs.)		4 kg (10 lbs.)		2 kg (5 lbs.)	
Tobacco Toxics	I smoke tobacco	More than 10 times/ week		1-10 times/week		None in the past 6 months		None in the past year		None in the past 5 years	
	I use drugs such as marijuana, cocaine	Sometimes								Never	
	I overuse prescribed drugs or over-the-counter medicine	Almost daily		Fairly often		Only occasionally		Almost never		Never	
	I drink caffeine-containing coffee, tea, or cola	More than 10 times/ week		7-10/day		3-6/day		1-2/day		Never	
Alcohol	My average alcohol intake per week is ____	More than 20 drinks		13-20 drinks		11-12 drinks		8-10 drinks		0-7 drinks	
	I drink more than 4 drinks on an occasion	Almost daily		Fairly often		Only occasionally		Almost never		Never	
	I drive after drinking	Sometimes								Never	
Sleep Seatbelts Stress Safe Sex	I sleep well and feel rested	Almost never		Seldom		Some of the time		Fairly often		Almost always	
	I use seatbelts	Never		Seldom		Some of the time		Most of the time		Always	
	I am able to cope with the stresses in my life	Almost never		Seldom		Some of the time		Fairly often		Almost always	
	I relax and enjoy leisure time	Almost never		Seldom		Some of the time		Fairly often		Almost always	
	I practise safe sex	Almost never		Seldom		Some of the time		Fairly often		Always	
Type of behaviour	I seem to be in a hurry	Almost always		Fairly often		Some of the time		Seldom		Almost never	
	I feel angry or hostile	Almost always		Fairly often		Some of the time		Seldom		Almost never	
Insight	I am a positive or optimistic thinker	Almost never		Seldom		Some of the time		Fairly often		Almost always	
	I feel tense or uptight	Almost always		Fairly often		Some of the time		Seldom		Almost never	
	I feel sad or depressed	Almost always		Fairly often		Some of the time		Seldom		Almost never	
Career	I am satisfied with my job or role	Almost never		Seldom		Some of the time		Fairly often		Almost always	

Step 1: Total each column									
Step 2: Multiply the totals by the number indicated	0		1		2		3		4
Subtotal									
Step 3: Add your scores across bottom for your grand total			GRAND TOTAL						

Scores: 80-100 excellent; 70-79 good; 60-69 fair.

From Wilson, Dr. Douglas. (1995). FANTASTIC lifestyle assessments. Hamilton: Department of Family Medicine, McMaster University. Reproduced by permission.

Physical Activity Readiness
Questionnaire - PAR-Q
(revised 2002)

PAR-Q & YOU

(A Questionnaire for People Aged 15 to 69)

Regular physical activity is fun and healthy, and increasingly more people are starting to become more active every day. Being more active is very safe for most people. However, some people should check with their doctor before they start becoming much more physically active.

If you are planning to become much more physically active than you are now, start by answering the seven questions in the box below. If you are between the ages of 15 and 69, the PAR-Q will tell you if you should check with your doctor before you start. If you are over 69 years of age, and you are not used to being very active, check with your doctor.

Common sense is your best guide when you answer these questions. Please read the questions carefully and answer each one honestly: check YES or NO.

YES	NO		
☐	☐	1.	Has your doctor ever said that you have a heart condition <u>and</u> that you should only do physical activity recommended by a doctor?
☐	☐	2.	Do you feel pain in your chest when you do physical activity?
☐	☐	3.	In the past month, have you had chest pain when you were not doing physical activity?
☐	☐	4.	Do you lose your balance because of dizziness or do you ever lose consciousness?
☐	☐	5.	Do you have a bone or joint problem (for example, back, knee or hip) that could be made worse by a change in your physical activity?
☐	☐	6.	Is your doctor currently prescribing drugs (for example, water pills) for your blood pressure or heart condition?
☐	☐	7.	Do you know of <u>any other reason</u> why you should not do physical activity?

If you answered

YES to one or more questions

Talk with your doctor by phone or in person BEFORE you start becoming much more physically active or BEFORE you have a fitness appraisal. Tell your doctor about the PAR-Q and which questions you answered YES.

- You may be able to do any activity you want   as long as you start slowly and build up gradually. Or, you may need to restrict your activities to those which are safe for you. Talk with your doctor about the kinds of activities you wish to participate in and follow his/her advice.
- Find out which community programs are safe and helpful for you.

NO to all questions

If you answered NO honestly to <u>all</u> PAR-Q questions, you can be reasonably sure that you can:
- start becoming much more physically active – begin slowly and build up gradually. This is the safest and easiest way to go.
- take part in a fitness appraisal – this is an excellent way to determine your basic fitness so that you can plan the best way for you to live actively. It is also highly recommended that you have your blood pressure evaluated. If your reading is over 144/94, talk with your doctor before you start becoming much more physically active.

DELAY BECOMING MUCH MORE ACTIVE:
- if you are not feeling well because of a temporary illness such as a cold or a fever   wait until you feel better; or
- if you are or may be pregnant – talk to your doctor before you start becoming more active.

PLEASE NOTE: If your health changes so that you then answer YES to any of the above questions, tell your fitness or health professional. Ask whether you should change your physical activity plan.

<u>Informed Use of the PAR-Q:</u> The Canadian Society for Exercise Physiology, Health Canada, and their agents assume no liability for persons who undertake physical activity, and if in doubt after completing this questionnaire, consult your doctor prior to physical activity.

No changes permitted. You are encouraged to photocopy the PAR-Q but only if you use the entire form.

NOTE: If the PAR-Q is being given to a person before he or she participates in a physical activity program or a fitness appraisal, this section may be used for legal or administrative purposes.

"I have read, understood and completed this questionnaire. Any questions I had were answered to my full satisfaction."

NAME _____

SIGNATURE _____   DATE _____

SIGNATURE OF PARENT _____   WITNESS _____
or GUARDIAN (for participants under the age of majority)

> **Note: This physical activity clearance is valid for a maximum of 12 months from the date it is completed and becomes invalid if your condition changes so that you would answer YES to any of the seven questions.**

 © Canadian Society for Exercise Physiology   Supported by: Health   Santé
Canada   Canada

PERSONAL FITNESS TEST RESULTS TABLE

Name:					
		Age:		Date:	

A. BODY COMPOSITION ASSESSMENT

Weight (kg)				
Height (cm)				
			Healthy	Unhealthy
Body Mass Index (kg/m^2)				
Waist girth (cm)				

Skinfolds (mm)	Trial 1	Trial 2	Trial 3	Average
Biceps				
Triceps				
Subscapularis				
Iliac crest				
Medial calf				
			Healthy	Unhealthy
Sum of five skinfolds				
Sum of two trunk skinfolds				

BMI and SO5S	points		
WG and SO2S	points		
Total	points	Rating	

B. AEROBIC FITNESS: MODIFIED CANADIAN AEROBIC FITNESS TEST (mCAFT)

Starting stage					
Heart rate		Count used: ❏ palpitation (10 sec) ❏ Heart rate monitor (bpm)			
	1st stage		5th stage		
	2nd stage		6th stage		
	3rd stage		7th stage		
	4th stage		8th stage		
Heart rate (Final bpm)					
Healthy Aerobic Fitness			Score		
			Rating		

C. MUSCULOSKELETAL FITNESS

	Trial 1	Trial 2	Max	Rating
Grip strength - Right Hand (kg)				
Grip strength - Left Hand (kg)				
Combined right and left max (kg)				
Push-ups				
Trunk Forward Flexion (cm)				
Partial Curl-Up (max 25)				
Vertical Jump Beginning Height (cm)				

	Trial 1	Trial 2	Trial 3	Max Diff.	Rating
Vertical Jump (cm)					
Leg power (kgm/sec)					

BODY COMPOSITION ASSESSMENT

Body Composition Assessment

Complete the following to determine a healthy body composition and record your results. Refer to Appendices A and B for determination of health benefit zones.

(a) Body Mass Index (see Exercise 10.3)

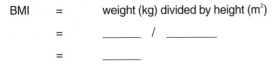

BMI   =   weight (kg) divided by height (m^2)

=   _____ / _____

=   _____

(b) Waist (Abdomen) girth (WG)

In a relaxed manner stand in an erect position with your hands at your sides. At the narrowing of the waist and at the end of normal expiration, position the tape to take a measurement.

WG   =   _____ cm

(c) Sum of five skinfolds (SO5S)

Refer to Figure 14.2 on page 213 of the text for an illustration of the five skinfolds to be measured. Complete one round of the five skinfold measurements before obtaining a second, and if the difference is greater than 0.4, do a third measurement and take the average. Be sure to take all skinfolds on the right side of the body and relax the muscles.

When the site of the skinfold has been located, use your thumb and forefinger with the back of your hand facing you to grasp the underlying fat. Always keep the calipers at a right angle to the body surface and note the measurement after the full pressure of the calipers has been applied to the skinfold.

Record your results directly in the personal fitness test table on page 146.

(d) Sum of two trunk skinfolds (SO2S)

Sum of two trunk skinfolds (SO2S) = subscapular + iliac crest

SO2S   =   _____ + _____

=   _____

AEROBIC FITNESS ASSESSMENT

Complete one of the following tests to determine your aerobic fitness and record your results.

(1) The Modified Canadian Aerobic Fitness Test

Refer to page 211 of the text for an overview of the test and an illustration of the stepping sequence. Refer to appendices C and D for the starting stage by age and gender and the ceiling post exercise heart rates respectively.

Use the following equation to calculate your aerobic fitness score and then refer to appendices E and F to determine your health-benefit zone.

Aerobic Fitness Score:

= $10\,[17.2 + (1.29 \times O_2\,\text{cost}) - (0.09 \times \text{wt. in kg}) - (0.18 \times \text{age in years})]$

= $10\,[17.2 + (1.29 \times \underline{\quad}) - (0.09 \times \underline{\quad}) - (0.18 \times \underline{\quad})]$

= _____

O_2 cost in ml/kg/min for different stages of the mCAFT		
Stage	Females	Males
1	15.9	15.9
2	18.0	18.0
3	22.0	22.0
4	24.5	24.5
5	26.3	29.5
6	29.5	33.6
7	33.6	36.2
8	36.2	40.1

(2) The 1.5–Mile Run

Refer to page 212 and Table 14.5 in the text for the testing protocol and estimated maximal oxygen uptake.

RESULT: Time _____;   Max VO_2 _____

(3) Dr. Luc Léger "Beep Test"

Refer to page 219 in the text for information regarding this test.

RESULT: Level _____;   Max VO_2 _____

MUSCULOSKELETAL FITNESS ASSESSMENT

Complete the following musculoskeletal fitness tests to determine your muscular strength and/or endurance and flexibility.

Refer to appendices G, H, and I to determine health-benefit zones for the musculoskeletal fitness tests.

(a) Hand Grip Strength

You will measure both hands alternately, in two trials. Grasp the dynamometer so that the second joint of the finger fits snugly under the handle and takes the weight of the instrument.

With a tight grip, hold the dynamometer in a straight-arm position away from the body and squeeze to exert maximum force. Exhale while squeezing.

Record your scores to the nearest kilogram and combine the maximum score for each hand on the results sheet.

(b) Vertical Jump

Note: If you suffer from any back ailment you should not perform this test.

Stand in an erect sideways position to a wall on which a measuring tape has been placed. To determine your beginning height, stand with your feet flat on the floor, reach as high as possible with your arms and hands fully extended, and your palm towards the wall. Have a partner record this height.

Next, assume a ready position with your hand on your hip and with your body a safe distance from the wall. Move into a semi-squat position (no pre-jump is permitted) and jump as high as possible with your arms fully extended, touching the tape at the peak height of your jump. Have a partner record this height.

Complete this three times and circle the highest jump on the results sheet. Between trials, a rest of 10-15 seconds is recommended.

To determine your height jumped in centimetres (max difference), subtract the beginning height from the peak height of the highest jump.

After completion of this test, use the following equation to determine your leg power and record your results:

Leg Power (kgm/s)

$$= 2.21 \times \text{weight (kg)} \times \sqrt{\text{vertical jump (m)}}$$

$$= 2.21 \times \underline{\hspace{1.5cm}} \times \underline{\hspace{1.5cm}}$$

$$= \underline{\hspace{1.5cm}}$$

(c) Push-Ups

Note: If you suffer from any lower back ailment you should not perform this test.

For this test, correct performance is imperative and the test is stopped when you are unable to maintain the correct push-up technique over two consecutive repetitions. Be sure to exhale on the effort phase of the push-up. The push-ups are performed consecutively, without a time limit.

- *Males:* Lie on your stomach with legs together and your hands pointing forward and positioned under your shoulders. Push up from the mat, keeping the body in a straight line, with elbows fully extended and using the toes as a pivot point. Return to the starting position with your chin to the mat. Neither the thighs nor stomach should touch the mat.

- *Females:* Lie on your stomach with your legs together and your hands pointing forward and positioned under your shoulders. Push up from the mat, keeping the upper body in a straight line, with elbows fully extended and using the knees as a pivot point. Return to the starting position with your chin to the mat. The stomach should not touch the mat. The lower legs, the ankles in a plantar flexed position, and feet remain in contact with the mat.

(d) Partial Curl-Up Test

Refer to p. 214 from the text for a description of the test. Use the cadence of 50 beats per minute on a metronome to set the rate of the curl-ups performed.

(e) Trunk Forward Flexion Test

Refer to the testing protocol on p. 215 from the text and record your results.

Jesse Palmer, 2002. AP Photo/Alan Mothner.

15

Biomechanical Principles and Applications

LEARNING OBJECTIVES

The exercises in this section of the workbook will help to reinforce your knowledge of the following topics covered in the textbook:

- The definition of the term "biomechanics" and its adaptation to exercise
- The contributions of Sir Isaac Newton to the field of physics and biomechanics
- The basic scientific models and theories used by biomechanics to describe and study human movement
- Linear and rotational motion
- The concept of the vector
- Lever systems and how they relate to the body
- The seven principles of biomechanics
- Applications of biomechanics to the world of sports, including the areas of performance improvement, injury prevention and/or rehabilitation, and fitness and/or personal training

EXERCISE 15.1
Section Quiz

MULTIPLE-CHOICE QUESTIONS

Circle the letter beside the answer that you believe to be correct.

1. **Force is a vector and is commonly represented using an arrow. Which of the following quantities is not a vector?**
   (a) 100 Newtons
   (b) 80 metres per second, North
   (c) 10 miles, East
   (d) 5 kilometres, South

2. **Which of the following concepts of rotational motion can be compared to the linear concept of mass?**
   (a) moment of force (torque)
   (b) angular velocity
   (c) moment of inertia
   (d) angular displacement

3. **The moment of inertia depends on**
   (a) the distribution of the mass in relation to the axis of rotation
   (b) the object's angular velocity
   (c) the moment of force
   (d) angular acceleration

4. **Force is a push or a pull of**
   (a) a certain magnitude in any direction
   (b) a certain magnitude in a particular direction
   (c) any magnitude, independent of direction
   (d) all the above

5. **When the resistance is between the force and the fulcrum, the type of lever is**
   (a) Class I
   (b) Class II
   (c) Class III
   (d) None of the above

6. **The product of force applied over a time interval refers to**
   (a) acceleration
   (b) momentum
   (c) impulse
   (d) none of the above

7. **By increasing the moment of inertia during a spin, an ice skater's angular velocity**
   (a) rapidly increases
   (b) decreases
   (c) remains the same
   (d) slowly increases

SHORT-ANSWER QUESTIONS

Briefly answer the following questions in the space provided:

1. Name and describe Newton's Three Laws of Motion.

2. List and describe the three classes of levers.

3. What are the four broad categories into which the seven principles of biomechanics can be grouped?

4. What does the principle of the application of force state?

5. What are the three key terms relating to angular motion?

6. What is the biomechanical formula for (1) force and (2) momentum?

7. What does the Conservation of Energy Principle state?

ESSAY QUESTIONS

On a separate sheet of paper, develop a 100-word response to the following questions:

1. Name and describe the seven principles of biomechanics.

2. Name and describe six applications of biomechanics.

3. With reference to the information box on the "Fosbury Flop" and the "jump serve," explain how biomechanics has played a role in advancing human performance in the high jump and volleyball.

EXERCISE 15.2
Terminology Review

DEFINING KEY TERMS

Briefly explain the meaning of the following key terms:

KEY TERM	DEFINITION
Biomechanics	
Scientific models	
Equilibrium	
Conservation of energy	
Newton's Three Laws of Motion	
Centre of mass	
Linear (or translational) motion	
Rotational motion	

Acceleration	
Force as a vector	
Angular acceleration	
Moment of force (torque)	
Moment of inertia	
Radius of gyration	
Classes of levers	
Applied biomechanics	
Seven principles of biomechanics	

EXERCISE 15.3

Crossword on Biomechanical Principles

Across

2. Developer of an innovative high jump technique
5. The product of an object's mass and its velocity
10. For an object to experience a change in momentum, this must be applied
12. Radius defined as the average distance from the axis of rotation
13. Common example of a winter activity involving a Class III lever
16. State of angular momentum when an athlete or object is freely rotating in the air
18. A landscaping tool that illustrates a Class II lever
20. Type of acceleration in rotational motion
22. Movement in a particular direction
23. Newton's Third Law of Motion
24. Mass times acceleration

Down

1. Levers are classified based on its location in relation to the force
3. Moment of force
4. The minimization of the surface area of an object in the direction of motion
6. Another name for "linear" motion
7. A measure of resistance to linear motion
8. Muscles that cross two joints
9. Field of science that studies how physical forces affect human movement
11. Newton's Second Law of Motion
14. A classic example of a Class III lever is the action involving this major joint of the upper limbs
15. Newton's First Law of Motion
17. Effect on angular velocity when an ice-skater increases the moment of inertia during a spin
19. Movement about an axis
21. Standard unit of measurement for force
22. What scientists ultimately strive for

EXERCISE 15.4

Measuring Human Motion

Determining and plotting the X and Y coordinates of joints reveals motion characteristics that can be used in the analysis of human movement. This exercise will familiarize you with the process of quantifying human movement.

DIGITIZING

On the next page are ten sequential photographs of a player kicking a soccer ball. To quantify human movement for analysis, the first step is to convert the visual images (pictures) into numeric values. This process is called *digitizing*, which simply refers to a method of obtaining an X and Y coordinate for each joint of interest.

Once obtained, these values can be used to create a stick figure plot of the movement. This representation can then be used in subsequent exercises to gain valuable information about the movement.

For this sample, obtain the X and Y coordinates for the hip, knee, and ankle joints for the right leg. Use your ruler to measure the X and Y coordinates of these three joints in millimetres for each picture (approximate if necessary). Use the bottom left corner of each figure as your graph origin and plot these values on the axes provided below.

Note the path of each marker. The foot goes through a much larger movement than the knee and hip. In fact, the hip moves only a small amount and mostly in the forward direction. In general, most physical movement involves large motion at the end of segments, while the joints closer to the body remain relatively stable.

Record the X and Y coordinates on this graph and join the lines for each separate image.

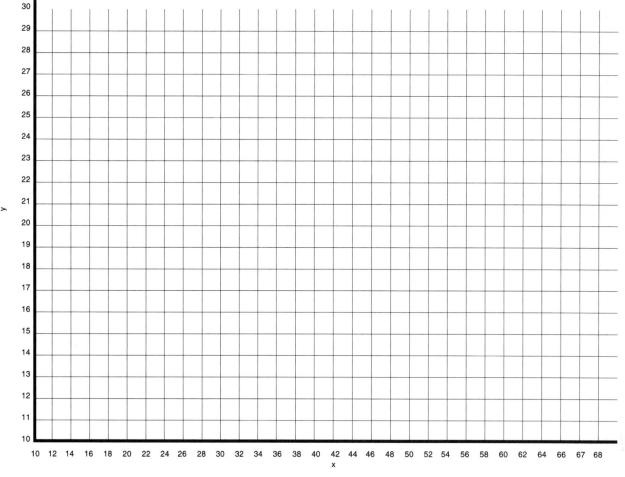

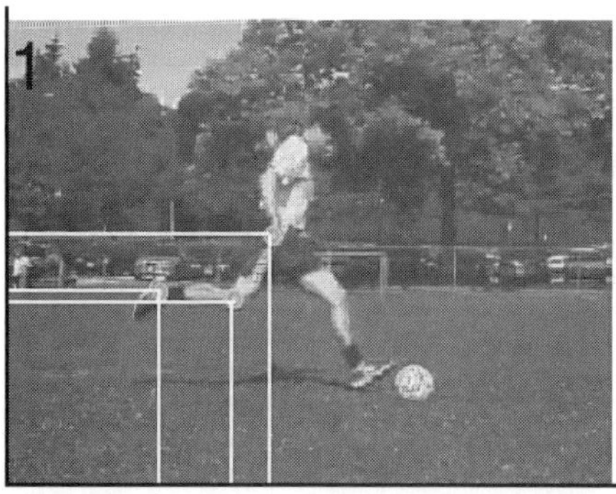

1

Coordinates in millimetres

	x	y
Hip	25	23
Knee	22	17
Ankle	15	18

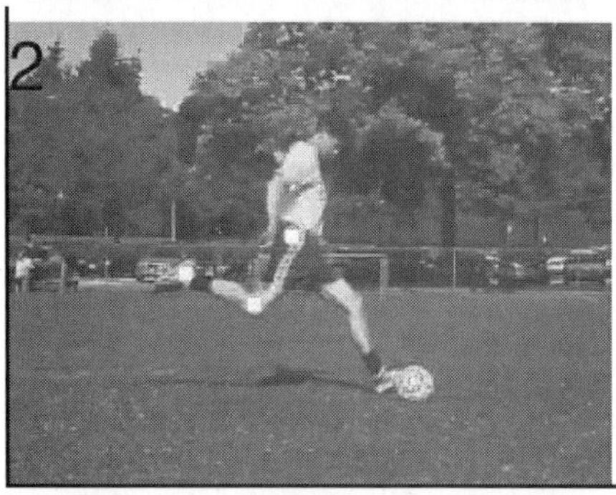

6

Hip   ___ ___
Knee   ___ ___
Ankle   ___ ___

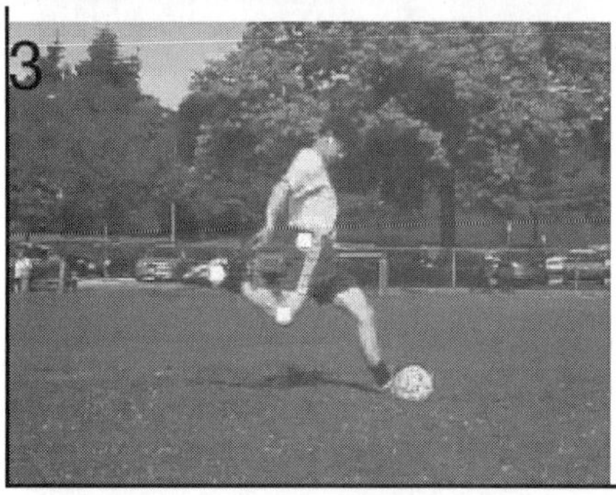

2

Hip   ___ ___
Knee   ___ ___
Ankle   ___ ___

7

Hip   ___ ___
Knee   ___ ___
Ankle   ___ ___

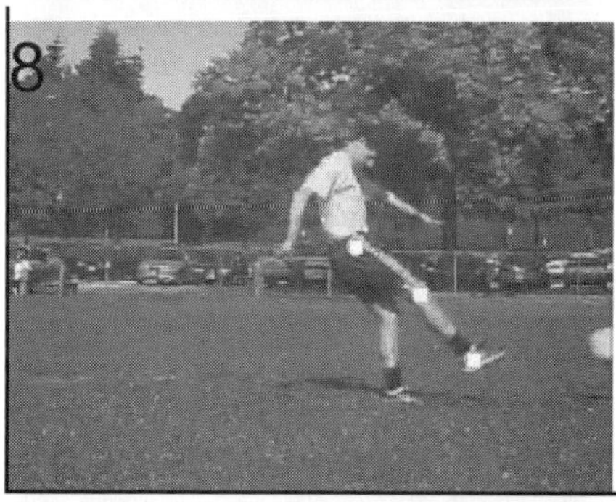

3

Hip   ___ ___
Knee   ___ ___
Ankle   ___ ___

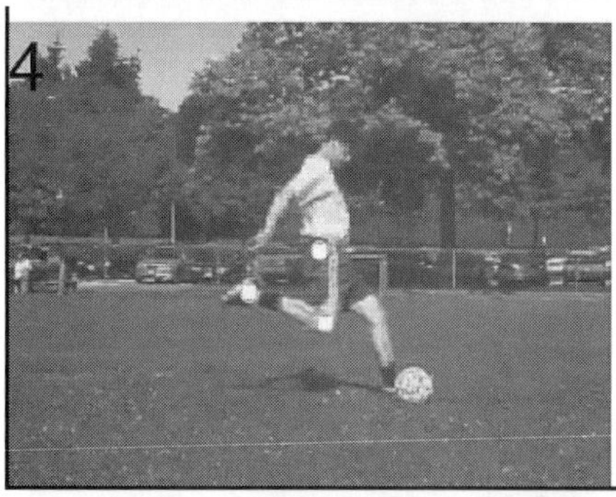

8

Hip   ___ ___
Knee   ___ ___
Ankle   ___ ___

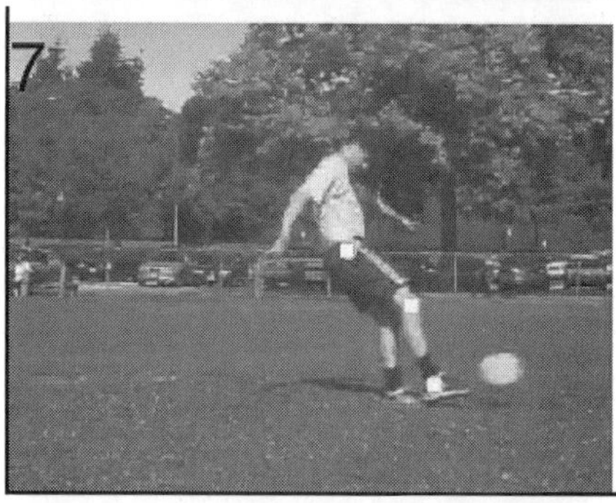

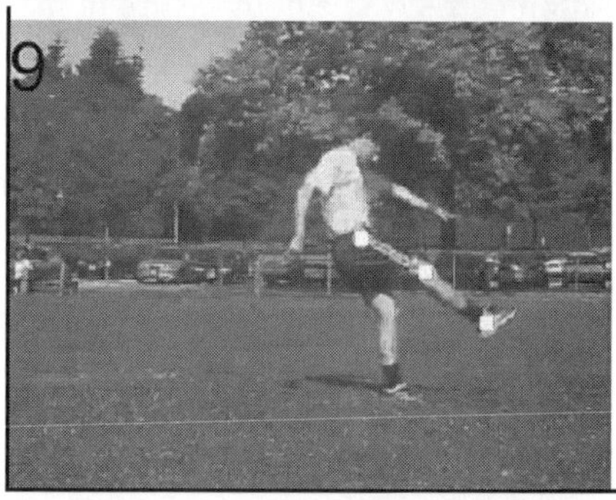

4

Hip   ___ ___
Knee   ___ ___
Ankle   ___ ___

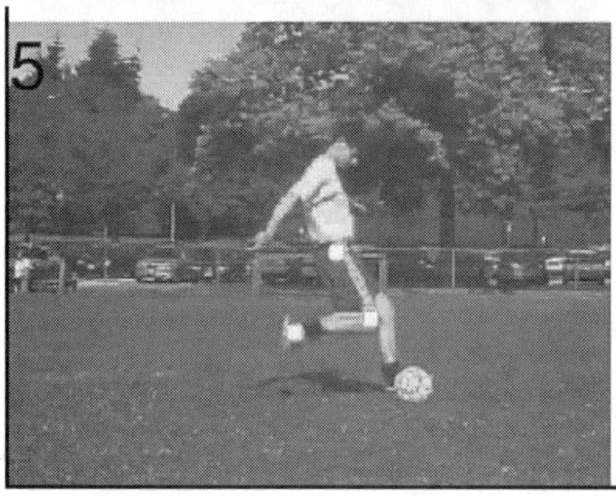

9

Hip   ___ ___
Knee   ___ ___
Ankle   ___ ___

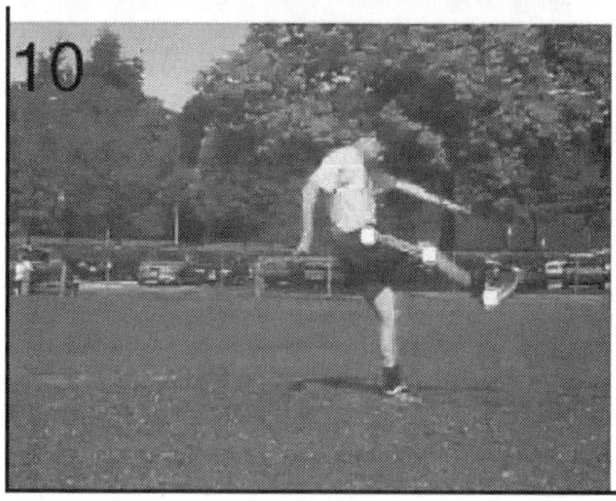

5

Hip   ___ ___
Knee   ___ ___
Ankle   ___ ___

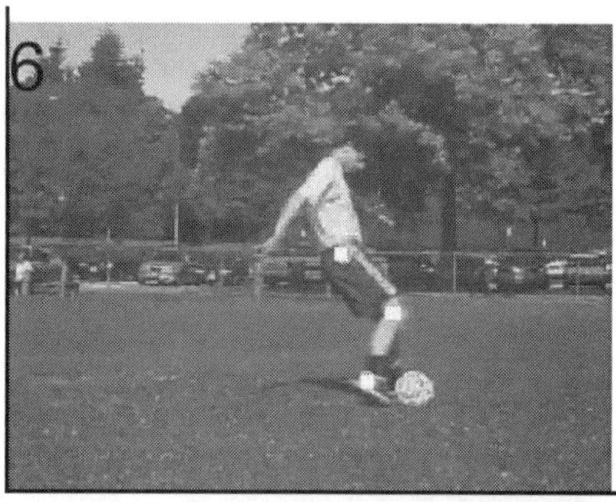

10

Hip   ___ ___
Knee   ___ ___
Ankle   ___ ___

EXERCISE 15.5

Determining the Position of the Centre of Mass

The segmentation method can be used to compute the position of the centre of mass. This exercise will acquaint you with how this method works.

CENTRE OF MASS

Can a resultant force such as gravity be considered to act through a single point in the body? The answer is yes and this point is called the *centre of mass*. If the object is of uniform density and shape, then this point will be in the geometric centre of the object. For other objects, such as the human body, we must use different techniques to find this point. The technique we use is called the *segmentation method*.

In this exercise you will use the segmentation method to compute the position of the centre of mass of the diver (below). To do this we must determine the position of the centre of mass of each segment with respect to the X and Y axes.

- **Step 1:** On the photograph on the next page draw a straight line over each of the following segments: foot, shank (lower leg), thigh, trunk, head, and left and right upper arm, forearm, and hand (as shown in the small drawing to the right). These lines then represent a stick figure of the diver and we can use these lines plus some other measures to determine the position of the whole body centre of mass.

- **Step 2:** Using the data in the second column of the table below, identify the position on the straight line for the position of that segment's centre of mass. For example, the position of the centre of mass for the thigh segment is measured as 37% of the distance to the hip end. Mark this location on the drawing.

- **Step 3:** On the large picture, using the lower left corner as the origin, measure and record the X and Y coordinates for each segmental centre of mass location. Enter the X coordinate in column B and the Y coordinate D respectively in the table.

- **Step 4:** For each segment, multiply the value in columns A and B and write this value in column C. For each segment multiply the value in columns A and D and write the result in column E.

- **Step 5:** Add all the values in column C and enter this sum in the bottom row. Do the same for column E. These two values represent the X and Y coordinates of the centre of mass for the diver. Plot this point (X and Y value) on the drawing.

Note: The centre of mass need not fall within the boundaries of the body. Rather, the position is dependent upon the orientation of the arms and legs.

SEGMENT	CENTRE OF MASS POSITION
Head	46% from vertex (top)
Trunk	38% from neck
Upper Arm	51% from shoulder
Forearm	39% to elbow
Hand	82% to wrist
Thigh	37% to hip
Calf (shank)	37% to knee
Foot	45% to heel

Canada's Larry Flewwelling competing in the diving event at the 1988 Olympic games in Seoul. CP PHOTO/COA/S.Grant.

SEGMENT	A	B	C	D	E
Head	.07				
Trunk	.51				
Right Upper Arm	.03				
Right Forearm	.02				
Right Hand	.01				
Left Upper Arm	.03				
Left Forearm	.02				
Left Hand	.01				
Thigh	.20				
Calf (shank)	.08				
Foot	.02				

EXERCISE 15.6

Joint Angles

The X and Y coordinates of joints can be used to compute a joint angle, an important component of human movement analysis. The exercise that follows will allow you to calculate these angles.

ANGULAR KINEMATICS

A useful means of displaying human movement is to determine the angle between segments. For example, the knee angle is the angle between the thigh segment (from the hip joint to the knee joint) and the shank segment (from the knee joint to the ankle joint). When you watch your friends walk or run, you can see that the knee joint angle sometimes becomes smaller (flexes) and sometimes, larger (extends). The phases of flexion and extension play an integral role in permitting humans to walk or run smoothly.

Using the stick figure data constructed in Exercise 15.4, you can determine the knee joint angle for our soccer kick. For each of the ten stick figures that you plotted, use a protractor to measure the angle between the thigh segment and the shank segment. Enter these values in the table. To determine the angle measurement, place one of the arms of the protractor along the shank segment and record the angle between that segment and the thigh segment (as shown in the drawing below).

Now that you have the table complete, you can plot the joint angle versus picture number. Knowing that each picture was made about 0.07 seconds (1/30th of a second) apart, you can actually plot the angle versus time. Graph your data on the chart provided on the previous page and compare your plot to the one provided.

ANGULAR DISPLACEMENT

In the plot you have created, you can see that the knee angle goes through some phases where the angle decreases and then increases. The phase where the angle decreases is called **flexion**. The angle is getting smaller so that the moment of inertia of the whole leg is reduced (see Section 15 of the textbook). This reduction in moment of inertia makes it easier for the athlete to develop high rotational velocity.

Once the knee has been flexed to a small angle, it is then extended to a maximum of close to 180°. This phase of extension results in a very high velocity of the foot which ensures that the force at contact with the ball is very large. Ensuring that these motions occur at the right time is a task facing all athletes.

Measuring the angular displacement of limbs and joints provides a key step in the analysis of human movement.

Joint Angle Versus Time: Compare your plot to this one.

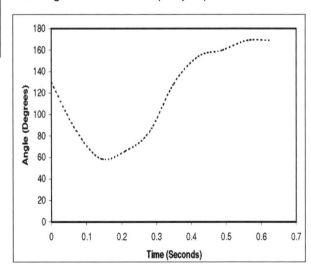

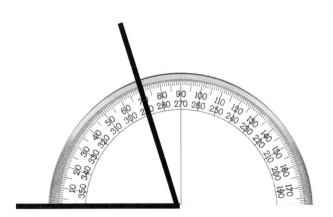

PICTURE NUMBER	TIME (SECONDS)	KNEE JOINT ANGLE
1	0.00	
2	0.07	
3	0.14	
4	0.21	
5	0.28	
6	0.35	
7	0.42	
8	0.49	
9	0.56	
10	0.63	

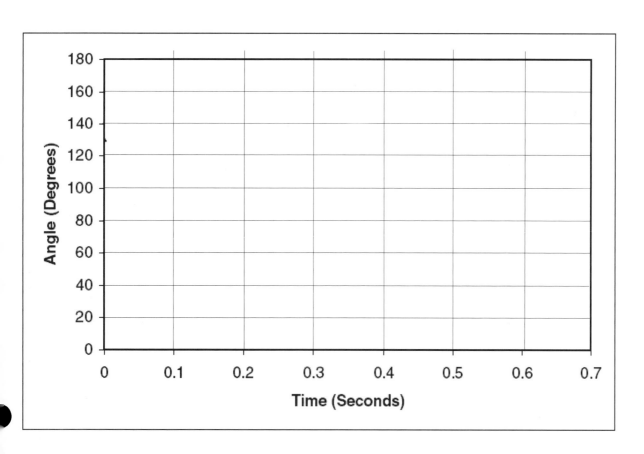

EXERCISE 15.7
Joint Angular Velocity

In the previous exercise, you computed and plotted the joint angle as a function of time. In this exercise, you will take the next step and determine the angular velocity of the joint. This process, called differentiation, can be done by drawing a set of straight lines tangent to the curved joint angle-time plot.

The slope of a curved line can be estimated by drawing a straight line tangential to the curved line at the point of interest. This would be termed the *instantaneous slope*. Another method is to estimate the average slope between points, thereby calculating an average velocity. Using either of these methods allows computation of the angular velocity of a joint from the angular displacement data.

In the small drawing below, the curved line represents an example of the angular position of the knee joint during a movement. To compute the angular velocity of this movement, first place two points along the curve. Then draw a straight line between these points. To compute the slope of this straight line, record the rise (change in joint angle, or Δ Angle) and the run (change in time, Δt). You know from your textbook that angular velocity is the rate of change of angle. Thus, by calculating the slope of this line, you have calculated the angular velocity.

As this is an average value of the slope, you must plot this half way between the two points. When you do this for a series of points, you can create a graph of angular velocity and time. Such data are very important to the biomechanist in the search for a deeper understanding of human movement.

The goal of this exercise is to determine the slope of the angle-time graph from Exercise 15.6. There are a number of steps to perform.

First, copy the angle data from the previous exercise into the second column of the table. Now, on the plot, in Exercise 15.6, draw a straight line between each successive point. For each of these lines, determine the rise (change in joint angle, or Δ Angle) and enter the value in the fourth column of the table. Because each point in your plot was exactly the same distance apart in time, the run for every point is the same (0.07 seconds). The final step is to divide the rise (Δ Angle) by the run (Δt) and enter these numbers in the final column of the table.

Once the table has been completed, you can create a new graph by plotting the point number and its associated velocity value on the graph provided on the next page. It should look like the plot at the bottom of the previous column.

Now that you have plotted the data, you should note how high joint angular velocities can be. In fact, in normal activities such as walking, the knee joint will reach peak angular velocity of about 300 degrees/second, and values as high as 2,000 degrees/second have been recorded in some martial arts movements.

Joint Velocities: Compare your plot to the one below.

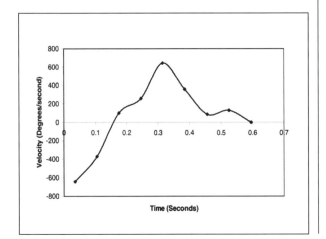

Calculating the slope.

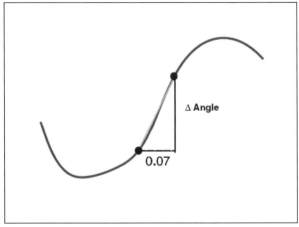

Time (seconds) from Exercise 15.3	Angle (degrees) from previous exercise	New time (seconds)	Δ Angle	Slope (Degrees/second)
0.00		0.000		
0.07		0.035		
0.14		0.105		
0.21		0.175		
0.28		0.245		
0.35		0.315		
0.42		0.385		
0.49		0.455		
0.56		0.525		
0.63		0.595		

Your plot.

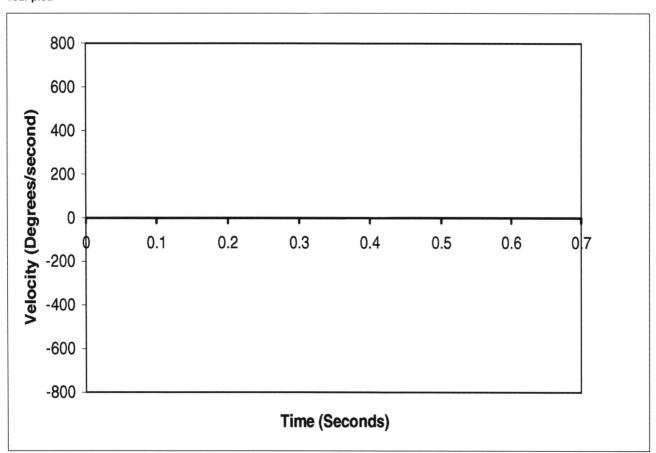

EXERCISE 15.8

Newton's Laws: F = ma

Sir Isaac Newton identified three laws that govern motion. These laws also apply to human motion. This exercise examines two of these laws.

When you walk, your feet land on the ground. When you are in contact with the ground, Newton's third law states that there will be a reaction force from the ground applied to you. In a biomechanics lab, we can record the force between your feet and the ground and use these recordings to help us understand the biomechanics of walking.

Consider watching a friend walk. He might look like the person in the picture on the next page. The three lines indicate the force between his left leg and the ground. The diagonal line is the resultant force, while the two other lines represent the vertical and horizontal components of that force.

If we record the forces, the graph would look like the one shown below. The top line represents the vertical component of the ground reaction force, while the bottom line represents the fore-aft component of the ground reaction force. The vertical component, of course, points upward all the time. If it did not, then you would fall to the floor. The fore-aft component is interesting because it points first negatively and then positively. According to Newton's second law, F = ma, this force would result in a negative acceleration in the first half and then a positive direction in the second half. This would mean that, for each step you take, you first slow down (negative acceleration) and then speed up (positive acceleration). Analysis of this type of data helps us understand how people walk.

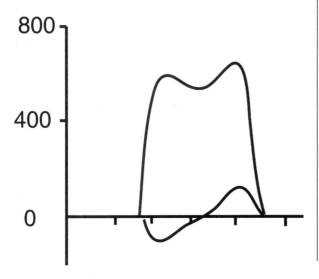

Linear Kinetics of Walking

In this exercise, you have two force-time curves, one for a person with a below-knee amputation walking on a prosthetic leg and one for an individual with two intact legs (the "control"). The plot shows the force-time data for the horizontal force – the fore-aft force as shown as the bottom line in the diagram on this page. The force is initially negative. The force then has a single moment when it is zero. The final phase of the force is positive.

Calculating Acceleration

You can calculate the acceleration of the individual if you know the mass and the force. Newton's second law states that

F = ma (which can be changed to **a = F/m**)

The control person had a mass of 62.69 kg while the person with the prosthetic had a mass of 69.72 kg. Using the force-time values observed at each stage of a stepping action, it is possible to determine the peak negative and peak positive acceleration of the person.

Sample Data

The full data set for this experiment consists of 100 observations over the course of one stepping action by each of the two individuals. From these two sets of observations, it is possible to compute acceleration at each stage and create a graph resembling the bottom line on the left. It is also possible to determine peak positive and negative accelerations for the two individuals.

To simplify, twenty observations from the full dataset are provided on the next page. (1) **Compute the peak accelerations using a calculator** and (2) **plot the resulting data on the graph on the next page** – it should resemble the lower line in the graph on the left.

Finally, it is interesting to note that the actual peak accelerations were smaller for the person with the amputation (as one might well expect). Why? Perhaps because he was not walking as quickly as the control person.

LINEAR KINETICS OF WALKING

Stance	Control person (with no prosthetic)			Person with prosthetic		
	A-P Force	Mass	Acceleration (a = F/m)	A-P Force	Mass	Acceleration (a = F/m)
1	6.571	62.69 kg		24.345	69.72 kg	
5	-30.34	62.69 kg		-28.217	69.72 kg	
10	-129.686	62.69 kg		-78.106	69.72 kg	
15	-161.108	62.69 kg		-120.814	69.72 kg	
20	-158.618	62.69 kg		-131.195	69.72 kg	
25	-119.965	62.69 kg		-99.507	69.72 kg	
30	-81.925	62.69 kg		-62.544	69.72 kg	
35	-51.458	62.69 kg		-35.848	69.72 kg	
40	-29.4	62.69 kg		-23.833	69.72 kg	
45	-13.097	62.69 kg		-17.516	69.72 kg	
50	-5.614	62.69 kg		-6.656	69.72 kg	
55	5.811	62.69 kg		6.194	69.72 kg	
60	20.603	62.69 kg		13.234	69.72 kg	
65	39.59	62.69 kg		18.183	69.72 kg	
70	76.468	62.69 kg		35.035	69.72 kg	
75	117.534	62.69 kg		62.141	69.72 kg	
80	148.851	62.69 kg		92.545	69.72 kg	
85	164.084	62.69 kg		123.814	69.72 kg	
90	136.533	62.69 kg		133.684	69.72 kg	
95	59.828	62.69 kg		106.535	69.72 kg	
100	7.166	62.69 kg		10.663	69.72 kg	

	Control	Prosthetic
Peak negative acceleration		
Peak positive acceleration		

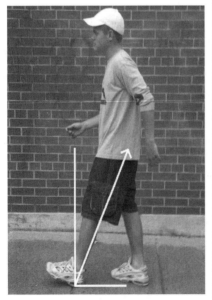

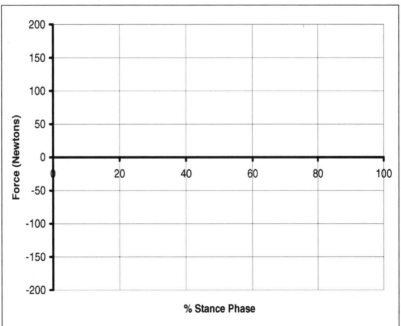

EXERCISE 15.9

Impulse-Momentum (FΔt = mΔv)

Newton's Second Law can be restated as the impulse-momentum relationship. In this exercise, you will discover the importance of this relationship as a tool for the analysis of human movement.

IMPULSE-MOMENTUM RELATIONSHIP

Newton's Second Law states that $F = ma$. That is, when a force is applied to an object of mass "m", it will accelerate and that acceleration will be proportional to the mass. That acceleration is the rate of change of velocity with respect to time, $a = \Delta v/\Delta t$. (The Greek symbol Δ is used to denote a change.)

With simple substitution, we see that $F = m(\Delta v/\Delta t)$, and when we multiply both sides by "Δt", we arrive at the impulse-momentum relationship, namely,

$$F\Delta t = m\Delta v$$

In words, this means that, when a force is applied over a time interval, "Δt", the momentum of the object (mv) will change. If the force is in the opposite direction from the velocity, then the momentum will be reduced. If it is in the same direction, then the momentum will be increased.

The average force of this collision can be determined from this relationship, where

$$F_{average} = mv_f - mv_i /\Delta t$$

In the analysis of sporting movements, this is a key relationship to understand.

AP Photo/David Zalubowski

HITTING A BASEBALL

Consider hitting a baseball with a bat. The bat is swung by the player, and when it contacts the ball, a force from the bat is applied to the ball that causes the ball to accelerate – that is, change its velocity. Because the ball was moving initially towards the batter, this acceleration will be in the opposite direction and be large enough first to stop the ball and then to continue accelerating it so that it flies to the field. In other words, there will be a change in the ball's momentum.

Now, consider a typical recreational baseball game. The pitcher throws the ball (with a mass of .2 kg) at you, and it is moving at 70 mph (110 kph). You swing the bat and strike the ball perfectly, hitting it to the outfield at a velocity of 75 mph (120 kph). The ball was in contact with the bat for only 0.8 msecs. **Using the impulse-momentum relationship, estimate the average force of contact and complete the table to the left.** (When you complete the table, you must convert the speed of the ball from mph to m/s.)

In fact, it amounts to a lot of force. Using Newton's Second Law ($F = ma$), you can determine that the acceleration of the ball is about 80,951 m/s/s − or 8,251 times the acceleration of gravity.

Mass of baseball (m)	0.2	kg		
Velocity of pitch (-v_i)*		mph (÷ 2.239)	=	m/s
Velocity of hit (mv_f)		mph (÷2.239)	=	m/s
Duration of bat-ball contact (Δt)	800	msec (÷1000)	=	s
Momentum after pitch (mv_i)		kg/m/s		
Momentum after hit (mv_f)		kg/m/s		
Average Force (mv_f - mv_i)/Δt		Newtons		

* Remember that because velocity is a vector it has direction and magnitude. Therefore, consider the velocity after the pitch as being a negative velocity and after being struck by the bat it will have a positive velocity.

EXERCISE 15.10
Work and Energy

The "Work-Energy Theorem" states that, when work is done on an object, there is a change in its kinetic energy. This exercise explores this theorem in the context of a car crash.

WORK-ENERGY THEOREM

When a force moves an object, we can say that work has been done. **Work**, then, is a measure of the force applied to an object and the distance over which the object moves (W = Fd). To do work, one must have energy. Thus, we say that **energy** is the capacity to do work. **Power** is the rate of doing work, or the rate of using energy (one must have energy to do work).

While energy comes in many forms, including heat and light, in biomechanics we are usually only concerned with **mechanical energy.** Mechanical energy includes potential energy and kinetic energy, which may be linear or rotational. **Potential energy** is the energy of position and is dependent upon acceleration due to gravity, the mass of the object, and the height above some reference line (PE = mgh). For example, a student with 50 kg mass standing on a 10 m high diving tower has more potential energy than the same student standing on a five-metre diving tower. **Kinetic energy** is the energy of motion and is a function of mass and the velocity of motion squared ($KE = \frac{1}{2}mv^2$).

In understanding the biomechanics of human movements, we often use the **Work-Energy Theorem**. This theorem states that, when work is done on an object, there is a change in its kinetic energy. To illustrate this relationship, let us consider an automobile accident.

A driver suddenly finds himself heading straight towards a large building. He or she does not have enough time to step on the brake and so runs straight into the wall. We can use the work-energy theorem to estimate the average force at collision.

The Work-Energy Theorem states that the change in kinetic energy of the vehicle will be equal to the

Understanding the large force values involved, imagine what happens to the driver if he or she is not wearing a seatbelt.

work done on the vehicle to stop it. In this example, the average force at impact times the distance over the collapse of the car would be equal to the change in kinetic energy. As an equation, this would be

$$F_{average}d = (\tfrac{1}{2}mv^2)_f - (\tfrac{1}{2}mv^2)_I$$

Let us use some values (see table below). The car was initially travelling at 50 kph or 13.9 m/s (1 kph = .2777 m/s), and after the collision, its speed was zero (it had stopped). Depending on the design of the car, the front end would collapse and the distance over which it collapses would determine the average force.

Let us say that the collapse is equal to 1 m. **(1) Calculate the size of the average force and record in the table** – it is easy to see why there can be so much damage to a car.

Now, **(2) choose your own car and substitute its mass in the table. Select the initial velocity and crush distance, and repeat the calculations.**

	(1) Example in text				(2) Your vehicle			
Car mass (m)	1,200	kg				kg		
Initial velocity (v_i) (use m/s value)	50	kph	=	13.9 m/s		kph	=	m/s
Final velocity (v_f) (use m/s value)	0	kph	=	0 m/s	0	kph	=	0 m/s
Initial kinetic energy ($\frac{1}{2}mv^2$)								
Final kinetic energy ($\frac{1}{2}mv^2$)								
Collapse distance (d)	1	m				m		
Average Force $F_{average}$ = (Initial KE–Final KE)/d								

Notes

16

Unit 2 Career Choices

Investigate a career in one of the fields covered in Unit 2. Ideally, you should interview someone working in the career for this assignment.

1. Career and description

_____
_____
_____
_____
_____
_____
_____
_____
_____
_____
_____

2. List at least two post-secondary institutions in Ontario and/or Canada that offer programs for this career.

_____
_____
_____
_____

3. Choose one of the above institutions and determine the required courses in the first year of study for this program.

_____
_____
_____
_____
_____
_____
_____
_____
_____
_____

4. What is the total length of the education needed to begin this career? Is an internship or apprenticeship required?

_____
_____
_____
_____

5. What is the average starting salary for this career? What is the top salary? On what do salary increases depend in this career?

_____
_____
_____
_____

6. What is the demand for individuals qualified for this occupation? If possible, provide some employment data to support the answer to this question.

_____
_____
_____
_____
_____
_____
_____

7. List occupational settings where a person with these qualifications could work.

_____
_____
_____
_____
_____

17
Unit 2 Crossword Challenge

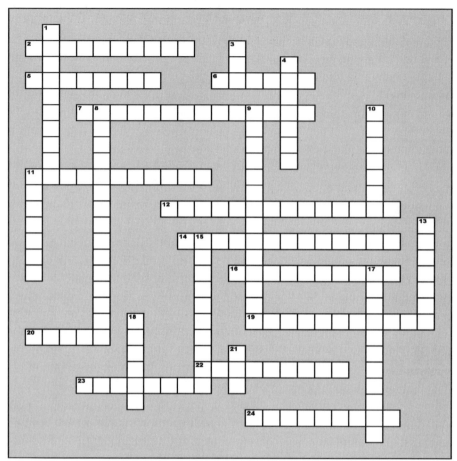

Across

2. Type of training that combines resistance and endurance training; also called cross-training
5. Another name for heart rate reserve method
6. Movement in a particular direction
7. Our direct sources of energy, consisting of carbohydrates, proteins, and fats
11. Term referring to the ability of a joint to move freely through its full range of motion
12. Type of endurance that is the best indicator of overall health
14. Term used to describe the breaking down of training into time-specific segments
16. Condition resulting from a complete failure of the body's heat-regulatory system
19. Dietary supplements that may contain hidden amount of steroids and other banned substances
20. He led inquiry into the use of illegal performance-enhancing drugs in Canada
22. Widely advertised as a "fat burner"
23. Performing this on motion helps athletes improve performance
24. Rate that measures the energy that needs to be consumed to sustain essential bodily functions

Down

1. Movement about an axis
3. Acronym for the ratio of a person's weight in kilograms to the square of his or her height in metres
4. Swedish word for "speed play" training
8. Process whereby the body adjusts to high altitude
9. Natural protein hormone produced in the kidneys
10. The moment defined as resistance to angular motion
11. Levers are classified based on its location in relation to the force
13. Users can interact realistically with this technological reality
15. Science sometimes called "human-factors engineering"
17. What a Calorie is also known as
18. Acronym for Canadian test that provides a simple, safe, and standardized approach to assessing major components of fitness
21. The maximal amount of weight an individual can lift for one repetition

UNIT 3

MOTOR LEARNING AND SKILLS DEVELOPMENT

Notes

18

Human Growth and Development

Wayne Gretzky, 2001. *CP PHOTO/Aaron Harris.*

LEARNING OBJECTIVES

The exercises in this section of the workbook will help to reinforce your knowledge of the following topics covered in the textbook:

- The four key components of human development: physical, cognitive, motor/skills, and social
- The relationship between age and physical development, and the various ways of measuring age (chronological, skeletal, and developmental)
- The study of human morphology and the three morphological types (mesomorph, ectomorph, and endomorph)
- The four basic stages of human growth and development: infancy/toddler; childhood; puberty/adolescence and adulthood
- The four basic phases of human movement: reflexive, rudimentary, fundamental, and sport-related
- The various rates of growth for different body parts, including the cephalocaudal and proximodistal sequences
- Various factors that influence physical growth, including glandular/hormonal activity, heredity, nutrition/diet, physical activity, and sociocultural factors
- Jean Piaget's "Four Stages of Cognitive Development"
- The stages of human social development, including tools for assessing this development in children

EXERCISE 18.1
Section Quiz

MULTIPLE-CHOICE QUESTIONS

Circle the letter beside the answer that you believe to be correct.

1. **Human physical development encompasses**
    (a) an individual's ability to interpret information
    (b) the ability to perform a wide range of tasks
    (c) relationship with peer, friends, and others
    (d) none of the above

2. **Skeletal age**
    (a) is indicated by the degree of ossification of bones
    (b) can be predicted according to chronological age
    (c) can be affected by diet, disease, and injury
    (d) all of the above

3. **Which stage of human growth witnesses the most rapid physical development?**
    (a) childhood
    (b) developmental
    (c) rudimentary
    (d) reflexive

4. **People are considered to "grow into their bodies" during**
    (a) the sport-related movement phase
    (b) puberty
    (c) the fundamental movement phase
    (d) adolescence

5. **Which system secretes hormones to the body's various organs and tissues?**
    (a) reproductive system
    (b) nervous system
    (c) endocrine system
    (d) lymphatic system

6. **The most accepted model of the stages of cognitive development was developed by**
    (a) Piaget
    (b) Erikson
    (c) Bandura
    (d) McLellan

7. **What is the greatest difficulty in trying to draw links between genetic heredity and growth:**
    (a) science has proven that there is absolutely no link between genetics and growth.
    (b) these links do not give sufficient weight to environmental factors
    (c) it is easy to offend people by trying to make such connections
    (d) in most cases, it is impossible to track growth patterns in large populations.

SHORT-ANSWER QUESTIONS

Briefly answer the following questions in the space provided:

1. **List the four key components of human development**

2. **What are the differences between chronological, skeletal, and developmental age?**

3. **Identify and provide a short description of the three classic body types.**

4. **List the four key stages of human development.**

5. **Describe how a lack of physical activity can affect human growth.**

6. **Who developed the four-stage model of cognitive development? What are the four stages contained in it?**

ESSAY QUESTIONS

On a separate piece of paper, develop a 100-word response to the following questions.

1. **Using the four basic areas of human development (physical, cognitive, motor skills, and social), pick any person you know (e.g., a friend, relative, classmate, etc.) and write a brief report about their current level of development within each area.**

2. **What are the three morphologic types? What is the benefit of using this system of body classification? Does it have any drawbacks?**

3. **Discuss the role that sport participation and team membership can play in social interaction and relationship building.**

EXERCISE 18.2

Terminology Review

DEFINING KEY TERMS

Briefly explain the meaning of the following key terms:

KEY TERM	DEFINITION
Components of human development	
Chronological age	
Skeletal age	
Developmental age	
Morphology	
Stages of human development	
Phases of human movement	
Factors affecting physical growth	
Cognitive development	
Piaget's four stages of cognitive development	
Socialization	

EXERCISE 18.3

Crossword on Human Growth and Development

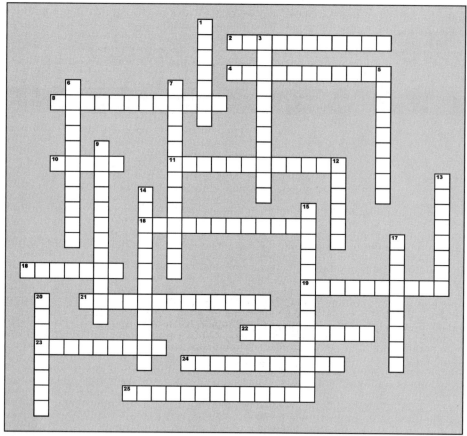

Across

2. Games held in the same year as the "regular" Olympic Games
4. A sumo wrestler belongs to this body type classification
8. For Piaget, this is the ability to adapt to one's environment
10. Type of development that combines cognitive and physical development
11. This can have an adverse effect on muscle growth and bone formation during childhood and adolescence
16. Stage defined by Piaget characterized by motor activity without the use of symbols
18. Stage of human growth that sees profound changes in human appearance (e.g., growth of body hair)
19. Categorization developed to help classify physical appearance and structure
21. Process by which humans form attachments with others
22. A diet lacking in these will impede growth
23. This period is relatively long in humans in comparison to other mammals
24. Movement phase in which humans begin to develop basic movement skills
25. Sequence in which growth progresses fastest in the head, followed by the trunk, and then the extremities

Down

1. Relative to other stages, the fastest growth occurs in this one
3. Basic activities such as crawling and walking develop during this movement phase
5. Development that includes awareness of one's self
6. Along with genetics, the major factor impacting human growth and development
7. Age as expressed in one's ability to perform certain tasks
9. Participation in team sports can further the development of this trait among young athletes
12. This process is usually complete by adulthood
13. Genetic lineage
14. As this process occurs, skeletal age increases
15. Sequence that describes how body movements originating close to the centre of the body seem to develop earlier than those farther away
17. Movement phase in which humans first show controlled motor development
20. Operational stage defined by Piaget in which logical thinking develops

EXERCISE 18.4

Motor Development Observation

An important concept inherent in motor skills development is that, within any given group of people, there can be a wide variation in development and skill levels. The following activity is designed to allow you to observe these variations in a small group.

OBSERVING MOTOR DEVELOPMENT

Arrange with your teacher for you to observe Grade 9 or 10 students during a physical education class in which the students will be learning and/or practising a sport or specific skill.

Select a partner. Then, at random and in agreement with your partner, select ten students in the class. Assign each of them a number or otherwise identify them. After you and your partner have selected your observation group of students and have agreed on your identification system, go to opposite ends of the gym.

Independent of your partner, observe your group of ten students "in action" for 30 minutes. (Remember to perform your observations unobtrusively and without consulting your partner. You will be able to compare notes at the end of the exercise.)

During your observation period, complete the table below as thoroughly as possible. Notes and observations should be detailed.

When you return to class, discuss your observations with your partner. Did you agree on your assessment of each student? Why or why not? What factors might explain some of the differences in assessment that occurred?

MOTOR DEVELOPMENT ASSESSMENT TABLE

DATE: _____

GRADE LEVEL UNDER OBSERVATION: _____

INSTRUCTOR FOR CLASS: _____

INDIVIDUAL (USE NUMBER)	1	2	3	4	5	6	7	8	9	10
Sport or skill(s) being practised										
Estimated height of Individual (Tall/medium/short)										
Estimated weight (Heavy/average/underweight)										

INDIVIDUAL (USE NUMBER)	1	2	3	4	5	6	7	8	9	10
Morphological type (Rough categorization) (Ectomorph – ECTO; Mesomorph – MESO; Endomorph – ENDO)										
Strength (Rate overall physical strength from 1 to 5 – weak to strong)										
Balance (Rate overall balance from 1 to 5 – very unstable to very stable)										
Coordination/agility (Rate overall coordination/agility from 1 to 5 – very poorly coordinated/ severely lacking in agility to very well coordinated/ extremely agile)										
Overall Skill Level (General rating of how well or poorly student performed the sport or skill from 1 to 5 – very poor to excellent)										
Notes on comparison with your partner during exercise										

EXERCISE 18.5

Adapting Sport Skills to Match Development Levels

There are many models available that describe how humans develop in well-defined stages. A related concept is that humans also develop in four interrelated ways — physically, cognitively, in terms of the motor skills they acquire, and socially. This exercise will allow you to become familiar with these aspects of human growth and development in a sports setting.

SKILL-LEVEL ADAPTATION

Imagine yourself as the coach of the group of athletes whose ages and sport are indicated on the chart below. Fill in as much information as possible about how you would endeavour to teach the sport skills indicated based on the appropriate age levels.

In each case, indicate how you would address the four developmental areas – physical, cognitive, motor skills, and social – and modify your instruction to the indicated age level. Keep in mind that you can modify equipment, basic rules of the sport, and many other factors in your attempts to match these activities to the appropriate age and/or developmental level.

Note: Assume that all of the athletes have "come through the ranks" of the various age levels – that is, a tennis player at Level 2 (aged 7-9) has already participated at Level 1; a soccer player at Level 3 (aged 9-11) has already participated at Levels 1 and 2, and so on. One entry has been completed to provide you with an example.

SPORT SKILL	AGE LEVEL	MODIFICATION
1. Hitting a baseball	Level 1 (under 5 years)	• use a "tee," as player of this age may have difficulty hitting moving pitch • use light bat to allow for lack of physical strength • work with the athlete to develop his or her swing without ball, encouraging him or her to "visualize" contact repeatedly • gradually introduce slow-moving pitch with larger ball for more advanced players • "social" aspects of this skill may be hard to develop as the skill is essentially individual
2. Kicking a soccer ball	Level 1 (under 5 years)	• • • •

3. Heading a soccer ball	Level 2 (5-7 years)	• • • •
4. Passing a hockey puck	Level 2 (5-7 years)	• • • •
5. Executing a cartwheel in gymnastics	Level 3 (7-9 years)	• • • •
6. Tossing a "spiral" pass in football	Level 3 (7-9 years)	• • • •
7. Executing a jump shot in basketball	Level 4 (9-11 years)	• • • •

19
Motor Learning and Skill Acquisition

LEARNING OBJECTIVES

The exercises in this section of the workbook will help to reinforce your knowledge of the following topics covered in the textbook:

- How humans acquire both simple and complex motor skills
- Basic principles of motor learning and skill acquisition
- Stages of motor learning, including Fitts and Posner's classic three-stage model
- Various factors affecting skill development
- Singer's five-step process to learning a skill
- The role of evaluation and feedback in learning a skill
- Skill categories, including locomotor, manipulative/handling, and stability-balancing
- Ways of analyzing and observing skills
- Adapting skill development to match a person's level of skill, including the processes of shaping and chaining

EXERCISE 19.1
Section Quiz

MULTIPLE-CHOICE QUESTIONS

Circle the letter beside the answer that you believe to be correct.

1. The process through which a person develops the ability to perform and refine a task or skill is commonly called
   - (a) physical development
   - (b) psychological development
   - (c) rudimentary learning
   - (d) motor learning

2. "Individuals differ widely in terms of how quickly and easily they learn new motor skills" defines the principle of
   - (a) motor development
   - (b) individual differences
   - (c) stages of learning
   - (d) skill development

3. What is the name given to the body's "mechanism" that coordinates the mental commands and physical responses needed to produce movement?
   - (a) effector
   - (b) decision
   - (c) memory
   - (e) perceptual

4. What do motor learning researchers consider to be the two basic divisions of motor activity?
   - (a) planned and spontaneous
   - (b) voluntary and involuntary
   - (c) psychological and physical
   - (d) instant and delayed

5. Feedback gained by knowledge of performance is also called
   - (a) knowledge feedback
   - (b) kinematic feedback
   - (c) performance feedback
   - (d) predictable feedback

6. The process of encouraging a learner to learn a skill gradually is called
   - (a) chaining
   - (b) linking
   - (c) shaping
   - (d) moulding

7. The two types of chaining are
   - (a) basic and advanced
   - (b) forward and backward
   - (c) critical and important
   - (d) beginning and automatic

SHORT-ANSWER QUESTIONS

Briefly answer the following questions in the space provided:

1. Explain the principle of individual differences. What factors can contribute to the way that this principle comes into play with people learning a skill?

2. What are the five stages in Singer's five-step method of skills teaching?

3. Why is skill transferability important when learning new skills?

4. What is the difference between open and closed skills?

5. Discuss how the chaining process can assist an individual to learn a more complex skill.

ESSAY QUESTIONS

On a separate piece of paper, develop a 100-word response to the following questions:

1. Outline the "classic" stages-of-learning model developed by Fitts and Posner and summarize each stage. Do you think this model accurately reflects the way people learn a new skill? Why or why not?

2. Choose one factor widely held to be an impediment to skill development, and describe a situation in which this factor is preventing an athlete from refining his or her skills in a specific sport. Suggest ways in which this inhibiting factor could be overcome.

3. Using a specific sport skill, describe how you would take a beginner through Singer's five-step approach to learn that skill.

EXERCISE 19.2
Terminology Review

DEFINING KEY TERMS

Briefly explain the meaning of the following key terms:

KEY TERM	DEFINITION
Motor learning	
Automatic/controlled motor activity	
Principle of individual differences	
Stages-of-learning model	
Factors affecting skill acquisition	
Five-step method of skills teaching	
Feedback	
Skill transferability	
Basic skill categories	
Open/closed skills	
Stages of skill observation	
Shaping	

EXERCISE 19.3

Motor Learning and Skill Acquisition

Across

1. The information a learner obtains regarding his or her performance
5. These supply the body with information regarding external stimuli
9. Singer's term for picturing the correct execution of a skill
11. This curve represents how well we learn a skill
13. Crowd noise is an example of this type of performance-inhibiting factor
16. Skill performed in an unpredictable environment
18. Movements needed to prepare for a skill
19. Physiologist who developed the two-dimensional system of skills classification
22. Skill development stage in which performance becomes "automatic"
23. Process by which instructors can assess the skills of learners
24. Skill development stage in which learners begin to refine skills
25. Term that describes how well we manipulate objects with our hands and feet

Down

2. Name for the mechanism that coordinates the mind and body
3. Motor activity that involves very little thought
4. Superstar who needed to refine important skill
6. Process by which learners are encouraged to develop a skill gradually
7. Co-developer with Fitts of the "classic" stages-of-learning model
8. Beginners make many; those at autonomous skill levels, very few
10. The first step in skills teaching in Singer's five-step model
12. "Keeping your mind on the game" is a popular way of expressing this key aspect of learning a skill
14. The instant at which a golfer's club hits the ball
15. Performing this when learning a skill allows you to understand what you are doing wrong
17. The ability to apply skills learned in one sports context in another sports context
20. Key mental function that allows us to recall past events
21. Motor activity that requires thought and time to perform

EXERCISE 19.4

Hockey Skills Observation

By breaking down the phases of a skill and analyzing them separately, coaches and athletes can look for ways to improve the execution of the skill as a whole. The next four exercises will allow you to become familiar with this process.

Skill Observation Checklist: *Using the photographs above, identify the key elements of each phase of the skill and indicate training exercises that might result in improvement at each phase.*

PHASE	KEY ELEMENTS OF PHASE	TRAINING EXERCISES
Preliminary Movements		
Backswing Movements		
Force-Producing Movements		
Critical Instant		
Follow-Through		

EXERCISE 19.5

Soccer Skills Observation

Skill Observation Checklist: *Using the photographs above, identify the key elements of each phase of the skill and indicate training exercises that might result in improvement at each phase.*

PHASE	KEY ELEMENTS OF PHASE	TRAINING EXERCISES
Preliminary Movements		
Backswing Movements		
Force-Producing Movements		
Critical Instant		
Follow-Through		

EXERCISE 19.6

Golf Skills Observation

Skill Observation Checklist: *Using the photographs above, identify the key elements of each phase of the skill and indicate training exercises that might result in improvement at each phase.*

PHASE	KEY ELEMENTS OF PHASE	TRAINING EXERCISES
Preliminary Movements		
Backswing Movements		
Force-Producing Movements		
Critical Instant		
Follow-Through		

EXERCISE 19.7

Tennis Skills Observation

Skill Observation Checklist: *Using the photographs above, identify the key elements of each phase of the skill and indicate training exercises that might result in improvement at each phase.*

PHASE	KEY ELEMENTS OF PHASE	TRAINING EXERCISES
Preliminary Movements		
Backswing Movements		
Force-Producing Movements		
Critical Instant		
Follow-Through		

20

The Psychology of Sport

LEARNING OBJECTIVES

The exercises in this section of the workbook will help to reinforce your knowledge of the following topics covered in the textbook:

- The basic principles and definition of sport psychology, including why psychological factors are important for athletes and coaches in both training and competition

- The relationship between physical and mental factors in sport

- How psychologists define performance states

- Key terms in sport psychology, including arousal, anxiety, relaxation, concentration, and motivation

- Psychological factors that can affect sport performance, including self-talk, imagery/visualization, hypnosis, the regulation of arousal and relaxation, motivation, goal setting and improving concentration

- The role of the audience and fatigue on an athlete's performance

- Orlick's "Wheel of Excellence"

- The impact of sport psychology on young athletes

- Various roles and careers open to sport psychologists

EXERCISE 20.1
Section Quiz

MULTIPLE-CHOICE QUESTIONS

Circle the letter beside the answer that you believe to be correct.

1. **Which of the following is a role of the sports psychologist?**
   (a) teaching an athlete how to block out crowd noise
   (b) working with coaches and athletes to improve motivation
   (c) helping competitors to avoid feelings of anxiety that inhibit performance
   (d) all of the above

2. **In the mind of the athlete, a complete absence of doubt, a narrow focus, a sense of effortlessness and the feeling that time has "stood still," describes**
   (a) "the zone"
   (b) ideal performance state
   (c) choking
   (d) both A and B are correct

3. **An athlete who, before a competition, is sweating or feeling "butterflies" is likely experiencing**
   (a) arousal
   (b) relaxation
   (c) anxiety
   (d) concentration

4. **Feeling "psyched up" or "wired" is known more formally in sports psychology as**
   (a) arousal
   (b) relaxation
   (c) anxiety
   (d) concentration

7. **An athlete develops a broad picture of what success "feels like" when using**
   (a) hypnosis
   (b) concentration
   (c) imagery
   (d) motivation

5. **Techniques for improving an athlete's concentration include**
   (a) positive self-talk
   (b) duplicating performance distractions in practice
   (c) use of cue words
   (d) all of the above

6. **Which of the following is *not* one of Orlick's seven key elements of excellence?**
   (a) confidence
   (b) distraction
   (c) focused connection
   (d) mental readiness

SHORT-ANSWER QUESTIONS

Briefly answer the following questions in the space provided:

1. **Define concentration and give three ways a person can increase their level of concentration during competitions.**

2. **Define motivation and discuss why some athletes are more motivated than others.**

3. **Why is goal-setting important for athletes? Why might objective or quantifiable goals be "better" than subjective goals?**

4. **What is "choking"? Why does it happen?**

5. **What are some important psychological points to remember when dealing with children in sports?**

ESSAY QUESTIONS

On a separate sheet of paper, develop a 100-word response to the following questions:

1. **Research any three famous athletes who have benefitted from using psychological practices, and explain how they used sport psychology to their advantage.**

2. **Imagine you are a sports psychologist who has been hired to work with a top-level athlete who has recently been "choking" in major events. Outline the steps you would take in working with the athlete to attempt to overcome this impediment to his or her performance.**

EXERCISE 20.2
Terminology Review

DEFINING KEY TERMS

Briefly explain the meaning of the following key terms:

KEY TERM	DEFINITION
Sport psychology	
Ideal performance state	
Arousal	
Anxiety	
Relaxation	
Concentration	
Motivation	

Role of the audience	
Fatigue	
Psychological skills training	
Self-talk	
Imagery and visualization	
Hypnosis	
Goal setting	
S.M.A.R.T. principle	
Wheel of Excellence	

EXERCISE 20.3

Sports Psychology Poster Exercise

Sport psychology is an area with many subfields, and it includes a wide range of techniques that are used to enhance performance. This exercise will enable you, in a group setting, to explore several of these aspects of sports psychology in greater detail.

CONSTRUCTING A SPORTS PSYCHOLOGY POSTER

To begin, form groups of students (maximum of 5).

Review Section 20 in your text to familiarize yourself with the key topics in the field of sport psychology. Each student in your group will select a different aspect of sport psychology. Research areas could include the following topics and strategies:

- arousal and relaxation regulation
- hypnosis
- self-talk
- concentration development
- motivation improvement
- imagery/visualization
- relaxation techniques
- fatigue
- any other suitable topic approved by the instructor

In the space provided below, and on a separate sheet of paper if necessary, compile notes about the aspect you have selected. Information should include a definition of the field, the fundamentals of how it works to enhance performance, people who use it (athletes, coaches, and psychologists), and real-life examples of how it has been used to assist athletes.

Each student will have one period to research their topic, either in the school library or Internet computer lab, and research can be completed at home or at an outside library.

After individual research is completed, reconvene with your group to compile your findings into a poster. Each of the topics should be represented on the poster.

Submit the poster to your instructor as a group (be sure to include the names of all compilers). All group members should also hand in their individual research notes for evaluation.

RESEARCH AREAS	INITIAL NOTES
Description of selected topic or strategy	
How the strategy is used	
Famous coaches/athletes/psychologists who use it	
When did it start being used?	
How it works	

EXERCISE 20.4

Sport Psychology — Annotated Bibliography

An annotated bibliography is a brief synopsis of books or articles that contains bibliographic information about their sources. In the following exercise, you will develop this type of document in the context of research on sports psychology.

COMPILING AN ANNOTATED BIBLIOGRAPHY

In this exercise, you will learn how to compile an annotated bibliography using articles that are available over the Internet.

Read the three online articles listed below. If possible, it is recommended that you print each of the articles into hard-copy format for further reference.

- **#1:** "What is sport psychology" www.spraguesportspsych.com (click article)

- **#2:** "Self-hypnosis for creative solutions" www.focusedtraining.com/a2.html

- **#3:** "Overcoming anxiety during competition" www.peakperformancepsych.com/anxiety.html

Find one additional article on your own using the following "Sports Psychology OverSite" website at:

http://www-personal.umich.edu/~bing/ oversite/sportpsych.html

Inform your teacher about your choice of article from this site. There are more than enough articles to supply a class. Students should hand in their selected article with the assignment.

Compile an annotated bibliography using the following entry as an example. Be sure to include the author, title of the article, and the name of the publication in which it appeared. Each entry should be no less than 70 words and not exceed 120 words, and should succinctly summarize the key points of the article.

Bibliographies should be typed using a 12-point font with 1-inch margins and be double-spaced. You can use the table below to outline your final report.

SAMPLE ENTRY

Lenihan, Brian P. (1996). A review of motivational practices among elite long- and middle-distance runners. *Australian Journal of Sport Psychology, 58* (1), 33-39.

This article examines, via a set of 40 interview questions, the motivational practices of 100 elite, long- and middle-distance runners at the Atlanta Summer Olympics in 1996. Author Lenihan surveyed an equal number of male and female runners and attempted to cover as wide a geographical/ethnic cross-section as possible, in order to establish preliminary data on whether or not motivational practices have a gender/ethnic basis. The author also provides data on how 'successful" each athlete's motivational approach was, based on their performance on the 1996 Games (athletes surveyed include a gold-medal winner).

AUTHOR, ARTICLE TITLE, SOURCE	SUMMARY IN POINT FORM
1.	• • • •
2.	• • • •
3.	• • • •
4.	• • • •

21
Coaching Principles and Practices

LEARNING OBJECTIVES

The exercises in this section of the workbook will help to reinforce your knowledge of the following topics covered in the textbook:

- The definition of the term "coach"
- Various styles adopted by coaches in pursuit of their roles, including authoritarian, business-like, "nice guy/gal," intense, and "easy-going"
- The differences between autocratic and democratic coaches
- The concept of "fair play" and its relation to coaching
- The roles and responsibilities of the coach in working with athletes
- The development of coaching skills
- How to build age-appropriate coaching strategies
- Guidelines for working with advanced athletes
- The differences between strategy, tactics, and planning in sport coaching
- The role of the National Coaching Certification Program in Canada
- Ethical and legal concerns for coaches
- How coaches and athletes can find the right working relationship
- Policies regarding the monitoring of coaches
- Opportunities for coaches in Canada

EXERCISE 21.1
Section Quiz

MULTIPLE-CHOICE QUESTIONS

Circle the letter beside the answer that you believe to be correct.

1. **When working with an athlete, which is the most important consideration for a coach?**
   (a) how working with the athlete will impact the coach's overall career
   (b) the athlete's commitment, in terms of time
   (c) whether or not the coach/athlete relationship will involve financial reimbursement for the coach
   (d) the athlete's age and ability level

2. **When attempting to select a coach, an athlete should ask about the coach's**
   (a) record with athletes of a similar background.
   (b) method of dealing with conflict
   (c) expectations for the athlete
   (d) all of the above

3. **Which coaching style best describes a coach who tells his team that he is not interested in any feedback about how a game is progressing?**
   (a) democratic coach
   (b) sympathetic coach
   (c) autocratic coach
   (d) business-like coach

4. **A coach who encourages a cyclist to take a short-cut during a race violates which NCCP philosophy?**
   (a) tactical decision-making ethics
   (b) the importance of coaching theory
   (c) knowledge of crucial coaching skills
   (d) fair play

5. **One of the significant things about Danièle Sauvageau's coaching success is that**
   (a) she has never played hockey herself
   (b) she has never coached Team Canada full time
   (c) she has never had an assistant coach
   (d) her teams never played together in non-Olympic years

6. **A coach and athlete who sit down to make a competitive plan before an event are engaged in:**
   (a) tactical planning
   (b) strategic planning
   (c) unfair play
   (d) poor sportsmanship

7. **Which best describes the role of the coach as outlined by the NCCP?**
   (a) gives positive feedback
   (b) builds an athlete's self-esteem
   (c) encourages participation
   (d) all of the above

SHORT-ANSWER QUESTIONS

Briefly answer the following questions in the space provided:

1. **Summarize the philosophy of fair play.**

2. **Choose three (of the eight) essentials of the role of the coach that you feel are the most important. Define each, and state why you think these three are the most important.**

3. **Which five skills or attributes are, in your opinion, the most important for a coach? Provide reasons for your answers.**

4. **Using your favourite sport, give an example of a good use of tactics by a coach and/or athlete, and one example of a poor tactical decision.**

5. **Define the term "ethical decision" as it relates to sport. List three ethical and three unethical decisions that could be made by a coach and his/her athlete.**

ESSAY QUESTIONS

On a separate sheet of paper, develop a 100-word response to the following questions:

1. **Discuss why there is a problem with the "win at all costs" philosophy when coaching younger athletes.**

2. **On page 286 of the text, a number of questions that an athlete might ask a prospective coach are presented. In your opinion, how would an "ideal" coach respond to three questions of your choice?**

EXERCISE 21.2

Terminology Review

DEFINING KEY TERMS

Briefly explain the meaning of the following key terms:

KEY TERM	DEFINITION
Coaching styles	
Autocratic coach	
Democratic coach	
National Coaching Certification Program (NCCP)	
Fair play	
Role of a coach	
Age-appropriate coaching strategies	
Strategy/tactics	
Standards of ethics and behaviour for coaches	
Coach-athlete relationship	

EXERCISE 21.3

Crossword on Coaching Principles and Practices

Across

2. The type of coach who involves athletes in most decisions
5. The bond between a successful coach and his or her athletes is based on this
6. Part of being a good coach and athlete is developing a sense of this towards the opponent
10. The type of coach who emphasizes discipline in practice and competition
14. Coaches with this type of attitude generally help young athletes to succeed
15. Working to maintain high levels of this is one of a coach's most important tasks
16. A more severe level of staleness
18. Coaches are often referred to as this by their athletes
19. The NCCP provides levels of this for coaches.
21. Name for the hands-on component of NCCP instruction for coaches
22. The practice of devising plans during actual competition
23. Deciding whether to use performance-enhancing drugs is an example of this type of decision
24. The type of coach who emphasizes winning above all

Down

1. Coaches can work to improve this by finding something to praise in every athlete's efforts
3. Coaches struggle with the decision to stress this over personal development
4. American coach who believed winning is "everything"
7. Allowing an athlete to determine aspects of his or her career fosters this
8. Under the fair-play philosophy, coaches must maintain this at all times
9. Most derive enjoyment and skill development from this
11. The practice of devising plans in advance of a competition
12. Former Olympic hockey coach; currently a police officer
13. An unpaid coach
16. Coaches who stress this see sport as only one aspect of life
17. The "do-as-I-say" approach to coaching
20. When coaching young athletes, building a relationship with these people is crucial

EXERCISE 21.4

Coaching Styles

Coaches at all levels of sport adopt a wide range of styles and approaches to working with athletes. In this exercise, you will assess which coaching styles, approaches, and philosophies are used by well-known coaches of top-level athletes.

COACHES AND THEIR STYLES

Select one of the well-known coaches from the list below (or one approved by your instructor) and on a separate sheet of paper answer the questions that follow. In most cases, additional research (on the Internet or in books and magazines) will be required.

- Jack Donohue

- Pat Riley

- Bobby Knight

- Phil Jackson

- Pat Quinn

- Pat Burns

- Bela Karyoli

- Vince Lombardi

- Chuck Daly

- Lou Pinella

- Bobby Cox

- Joe Torre

- Steve Mariucci

- Bill Parcells

- Pat Head Summit

- Danièle Sauvageau

- Any other coach approved by your instructor

QUESTIONS

1. For what sport is this coach best known?

2. Which one of the coaching styles outlined in the text does he or she demonstrate?

3. Is this coach best described as autocratic or democratic?

4. How does this coach motivate his or her athletes? Provide examples from actual competitions to support your answer.

5. Based on the discussion in the text about fair play and the ethical behaviour of coaches, would you say that this coach deals with matters in a fair and ethical manner? Again, give examples to justify your answers.

6. Indicate one instance in which this coach utilized a superior knowledge of strategies or tactics to the benefit of his or her athlete(s) in a competitive situation. Provide a brief description of when this happened.

7. If you were an athlete, would you like to work with the coach you selected? Why, or why not?

8. If you were a coach, would you attempt to emulate the coach you have chosen? Why, or why not?

EXERCISE 21.5
Coaching Comparison

Coaches use different techniques to elicit the best performance from athletes. In the following exercise, you will be asked to observe several coaches as they work with athletes to ascertain which techniques and approaches they use to conduct practice sessions.

COMPARING COACHING STYLES

With the approval of your teacher, attend a practice run by two different coaches. (It is also necessary to obtain approval from both of these coaches.)

The actual sport being coached or practiced does not matter – the two coaches can be involved in the same sport or different sports.

As you observe the practice sessions, complete the following charts by placing a check mark in the box beside the appropriate coaching style each time you see that style exhibited by the coach.

It may be that each coach will have a well-defined style, so do not be surprised if one box ends up being filled with a large number of check marks.

COACH'S NAME _____

SPORT _____

AGE LEVEL OF ATHLETE(S) _____

COACHING STYLE	DEFINITION	COACH 1	COACH 2
Authoritarian			
Business-Like			
Nice Guy/Gal			
Intense			
Easy-Going			

22

Unit 3 Career Choices

Investigate a career in one of the fields covered in Unit 3. Ideally, you should interview someone working in the career for this assignment.

1. Career and description

_____
_____
_____
_____
_____
_____
_____
_____
_____
_____
_____

2. List at least two post-secondary institutions in Ontario and/or Canada that offer programs for this career.

_____
_____
_____
_____

3. Choose one of the above institutions and determine the required courses in the first year of study for this program.

_____
_____
_____
_____
_____
_____
_____
_____
_____

4. What is the total length of the education needed to begin this career? Is an internship or apprenticeship required?

_____
_____
_____
_____

5. What is the average starting salary for this career? What is the top salary? On what do salary increases depend in this career?

_____
_____
_____
_____

6. What is the demand for individuals qualified for this occupation? If possible, provide some employment data to support the answer to this question.

_____
_____
_____
_____
_____
_____

7. List occupational settings where a person with these qualifications could work.

_____
_____
_____
_____

23

Unit 3 Crossword Challenge

Across

2. Type of learning in which a person develops the ability to perform a task
3. Classification of skill performed in stationary environmental conditions
4. Motor activity that involves very little thought
6. Ethical and behavioural rules set by most sport leagues and associations for coaches
8. Psychological state in which an athlete feels ready to do his or her very best in competition
10. Information a learner obtains regarding how he or she is progressing in learning to perform a skill
12. Acronym for instructional courses offered by the Coaching Association of Canada
15. Performance state commonly known as "the zone"
16. The ability to use a skill learned in one sport context in another sport context
17. Process in which learners develop a skill gradually
18. Coach who encourages his or her athletes to be fully involved in decisions
21. Process in which humans form attachments to others
22. What Robert Singer's five-step method was created to teach
23. Motor activity that needs thought and time to perform

Down

1. Acronym for basic framework for establishing goals
3. Process in which complex skills are broken into separate and distinct parts
5. Categorization created by researchers to help classify people's appearance and physical structure
6. Age indicated by physical maturity of the skeleton
7. Age expressed by one's ability to perform certain tasks
9. Coach who adopts a "do-as-I-say" approach
11. Type of play that is one of the fundamental tenets of the National Coaching Certification Program
13. Age measured in years, months, and days
14. Psychological process in which athletes imagine themselves succeeding
19. How a coach or a teacher evaluates an athlete's skills
20. Development characterized by changes in a person's ability to interpret and process information

---

UNIT 4

THE EVOLUTION OF PHYSICAL ACTIVITY AND SPORT

Notes

Former Edmonton Grads Margaret MacBurney Vasheresse and Helen Northup Alexander. CP PHOTO/John Ulan.

24
History of Physical Education and Sport

LEARNING OBJECTIVES

The exercises in this section of the workbook will help to reinforce your knowledge of the following topics covered in the textbook:

- Basic trends in sport history
- The role of the Greeks and Romans in sport development
- Sport in the Americas
- The European legacy of sport, including the importance of the Victorian era
- Racially segregated and restricted sport
- Canadians who have excelled in Olympic competition
- Early Canadian sport pioneers
- The rise of North American pro sport leagues
- Major twentieth-century achievements by Canadians in sport
- The importance of the Commonwealth Games
- The development of physical education in Canadian schools and society
- How sport and physical activity have contributed to Canadian society
- The concepts of exploitation and sport equity

© Copyright. It is illegal to photocopy without permission.

24. History of Physical Education and Sport • 203

EXERCISE 24.1
Section Quiz

MULTIPLE-CHOICE QUESTIONS

Circle the letter beside the answer that you believe to be correct.

1. **What is the Olympic Peace?**
   (a) offerings all athletes had to bring in order to be allowed to compete
   (b) ceremonial clothing worn by early Olympians
   (c) truce called in order to allow athletes to travel to Olympia
   (d) the prize offered to victorious athletes in early Olympic competition

2. **Physical education classes for children were instituted in 1420 in Europe by**
   (a) Leonardo da Vinci
   (b) Pierre de Coubertin
   (c) Queen Victoria
   (d) an Italian physician

3. **The Victorian gentleman athlete embraced the concepts of**
   (a) fair play
   (b) amateurism
   (c) sport as a reflection of life
   (d) all of the above

4. **Canadian winners at the Olympics include**
   (a) Gaetan Boucher
   (b) Tom Longboat
   (c) Edward "Ned" Hanlan
   (d) George Beers

5. **Professional teams arose when**
   (a) amateurism was no longer valued
   (b) teams started paying their best players to ensure patrons returned
   (c) Olympic sports became open to the common man
   (d) the Victorian age was at its height

6. **Which Canadian athlete was nicknamed the "Saskatoon Lily"?**
   (a) Elizabeth Manley
   (b) Nancy Greene
   (c) Barbara Ann Scott
   (d) Ethel Catherwood

7. **The Canadian hockey players who participated in games against the USSR represented**
   (a) the free-market capitalist society
   (b) the hopes and dreams of many Canadian youth
   (c) warriors in a clash of sporting ideologies
   (d) all of the above

SHORT-ANSWER QUESTIONS

Briefly answer the following questions in the space provided:

1. **Did Greek and Roman concepts of sport have any effect on each other? If so, what was it?**

2. **Define the concept of the "Renaissance man."**

3. **Why did the Victorians believe that participation in sports was harmful for women?**

4. **For what reasons did the NBA's Vancouver Grizzlies fail?**

5. **In what ways do the Canada Games serve young Canadian athletes?**

6. **Why is the principle of "equal access" an important concept in the world of sports?**

ESSAY QUESTIONS

On a separate piece of paper, develop a 100-word response to the following questions:

1. **Examine the Victorian beliefs with regard to sport.**

2. **What did the Olympic Charter emphasize? How did this affect the goals of the Olympic Movement?**

3. **Discuss the positive and negative aspects of athletes serving as role models for youth.**

EXERCISE 24.2
Terminology Review

DEFINING KEY TERMS

Briefly explain the meaning of the following key terms:

KEY TERM	DEFINITION
Olympic Games	
Renaissance man	
Calisthenics	
Olympic Charter	
Olympic Movement	
International Olympic Committee	
National Hockey League	

Edmonton Commercial Graduates Basketball Club	
Canadian Football League	
Commonwealth Games	
Canada Games	
Crazy Canucks	
ParticipAction	
Marathon of Hope	
Terry Fox Run	
Man in Motion World Tour	
Role models	
Exploitation	
Sport equity	

EXERCISE 24.3
Modern Olympic Timeline

Since their founding in 1896, the modern Olympic Games have been profoundly affected by political events. As well, they have provided chances for Canadian athletes to shine on the international sporting stage. In the following exercise, you will examine both of these important aspects of the modern Olympics.

OLYMPIC RESEARCH CHART

Fill in the charts below, providing significant political events surrounding the event (if any) and Canadian athletes who won at the Games (include event and medal awarded).

SUMMER OLYMPICS		POLITICAL EVENTS	CANADIAN MEDALISTS
1896	Athens, Greece		
1900	Paris, France		
1904	St. Louis, USA		
1906	Athens, Greece		
1908	London, England		
1912	Stockholm, Sweden		
1916	Not held (World War I)		
1920	Antwerp, Belgium		
1924	Paris, France		
1928	Amsterdam, The Netherlands		
1932	Los Angeles, USA		
1936	Berlin, Germany		
1940	Not held (World War II)		
1944	Not held (World War II)		
1948	London, England		
1952	Helsinki, Finland		
1956	Melbourne, Australia		
1960	Rome, Italy		
1964	Tokyo, Japan		
1968	Mexico City, Mexico		

1972	Munich, Germany		
1976	Montreal, Canada		
1980	Moscow, USSR		
1984	Los Angeles, USA		
1988	Seoul, South Korea		
1992	Barcelona, Spain		
1996	Atlanta, USA		
2000	Sydney, Australia		

WINTER OLYMPICS		POLITICAL EVENTS	CANADIAN MEDALISTS
1924	Chamonix, France		
1928	St. Moritz, Switzerland		
1932	Lake Placid, USA		
1936	Garmisch-Partenkirchen, Germany		
1948	St. Moritz, Switzerland		
1952	Oslo, Norway		
1956	Cortina d'Ampezzo, Italy		
1960	Squaw Valley, USA		
1964	Innsbruck, Austria		
1968	Genoble, France		
1972	Sapporo, Japan		
1976	Innsbruck, Austria		
1980	Lake Placid, USA		
1984	Sarajevo, Yugoslavia		
1988	Calgary, Canada		
1992	Albertville, France		
1994	Lillehammer, Norway		
1998	Nagano, Japan		
2002	Salt Lake City, USA		

EXERCISE 24.4

Canadian Sport Heroes and Their Achievements

Understanding the historical context of sport and physical activity can further your appreciation of current trends and events. The following exercise will acquaint you with the significant contribution made by Canadians in the history of sport.

THE ACHIEVEMENTS OF CANADIANS

Research the achievements of the following historical sport figures, using library and Internet resources, and fill in the chart below. (For your reference, the key dates of their major sporting achievements or the approximate period of their athletic activity follows their names.)

ATHLETE	ACHIEVEMENTS
James Naismith 1891	
Billy Sherring 1900 - 1910	
Tom Longboat 1905 - 1915	
Bobby (Fanny) Rosenfeld 1920s	
Velma Springstead 1920s	

Dorothy Prior 1920s	
Ethel Catherwood 1920s	
Alexandrine Gibb 1920s - 1930s	
Barbara Ann Scott 1940s	
Norm Kwong 1950s - 1960s	
Russ Jackson 1950s - 1960s	
Arnie Boldt 1960s - 1970s	
Nancy Greene 1960s - 1970s	

Bobby Orr 1960s - 1970s	
Carling Bassett-Seguso 1980s	
Gaetan Boucher 1980s	
Terry Fox 1980s	
Charmaine Crooks 1980s - 1990s	
Bruny Surin 1980s - 1990s	
Gary and Paul Gates 1980s - 1990s	
Wayne Gretzky 1980s - present	

Abby Hoffman 1980s - present	
Vicki Keith 1980s - present	
Teddy Nolan 1980s - present	
Sonia Denoncourt 1990s - present	
Hayley Wickenheiser 1990s - present	
Clara Hughes 1990s - present	
Marnie McBean 1990s - present	
Simon Whitfield 2000 - present	

Kara Lang. 2002. CP Photo/Adrian Wyld.

25
Women in Sport

LEARNING OBJECTIVES

The exercises in this section of the workbook will help to reinforce your knowledge of the following topics covered in the textbook:

- Basic trends and key events in the history of women in sport
- The growth of the Women's Amateur Athletic Federation
- Pioneering Canadian sportswomen
- The role of Title IX in women's sport
- The role of women in sport today
- Key athletes and events in contemporary Canadian women's sports
- Women in key positions in Canadian sports
- The media's impact on women in sport
- The concept of body image and its influence on women athletes
- The "female triad" and the dangers it poses
- The role of the Canadian Association for the Advancement of Women in Sport (CAAWS)

EXERCISE 25.1
Section Quiz

MULTIPLE-CHOICE QUESTIONS

Circle the letter beside the answer that you believe to be correct.

1. **In the 1920s, women participating in sport were still fighting for the right to**
   (a) wear sleeveless shirts
   (b) wear shorts
   (c) bare their legs
   (d) all of the above

2. **A landmark sexual discrimination case in the Supreme Court was won by**
   (a) Justine Blainey
   (b) Manon Rheaume
   (c) Hayley Wickenheiser
   (d) Alison Sydor

3. **Gender discrimination of any kind is prohibited in schools in the United by States by**
   (a) Educational Amendments
   (b) American Sport Policy
   (c) U.S. Charter of Rights and Freedoms
   (d) Title IX

4. **The Scott Tournament of Hearts**
   (a) is the Canadian Women's Curling Championship
   (b) won a Gemini award in 2001 for the best live sporting event
   (c) has been won five times by Colleen Jones
   (d) all of the above

5. **The majority of Canadian female sports teams**
   (a) are coached by women
   (b) are officiated by women
   (c) are coached by men
   (d) are coached by former female athletes

6. **The female triad can be broken by**
   (a) early identification and intervention
   (b) expressing general concern for the individual's health
   (c) seeking the guidance of trained medical professionals
   (d) all of the above

7. **The handbook and website *Speak Out! Act Now!* was released by**
   (a) the Canadian Association for the Advancement of Women
   (b) the Coaching Association of Canada
   (c) the Harassment and Abuse in Sport Collective
   (d) the Canadian Centre for Ethics in Sport

SHORT-ANSWER QUESTIONS

Briefly answer the following questions in the space provided:

1. **Which sport offers three inspiring tales of women who were allowed to compete successfully against men?**

2. **At which university was the first Physical Education Bachelor's Degree created? When?**

3. **Which federation merged with the Amateur Athletic Union of Canada?**

4. **Which female athlete cut off her hair and posed as a boy to join a hockey team?**

5. **What initiative was developed by the Canadian Heritage Ministry and released in 2002?**

6. **Which national women's team competed in the Women's Pacific Rim Championships?**

7. **What is needed to encourage women to enter leadership positions in sport?**

ESSAY QUESTIONS

On a separate piece of paper, develop a 100-word response to the following questions:

1. **Discuss the effects of Title IX for both American and Canadian female athletes.**

2. **Examine the issue of media coverage of women's sports. Discuss how it could be improved.**

3. **How has the Canadian Association for the Advancement of Women in Sport increased the rate of participation of girls and women in sport?**

EXERCISE 25.2
Terminology Review

DEFINING KEY TERMS

Briefly explain the meaning of the following key terms:

KEY TERM	DEFINITION
Femininity	
Women's Amateur Athletic Federation	
Title IX	
Gender representation in leadership positions	
Media coverage of women's sports	
Body image	
Female triad	
Canadian Association for the Advancement of Women in Sport (CAAWS)	
On The Move	
ACTive	
Girls @ Play	

EXERCISE 25.3

Crossword on Women in Sport

Across

1. This athlete turned from speed skating to cycling and then back to speed skating
2. Acronym for the first national body commonly called the Canadian Parliament of Women's Sport
3. Top athlete who became columnist
5. Head coach of Team Canada in hockey for the 2002 Winter Olympics
6. Clothing invented to aid female sports participation
9. Title of American equal-opportunity legislation that affects both U.S. and Canadian athletes
13. Petitclerc won this 800-metre race included in the 2002 Commonwealth Games
15. Acronym for organization that promotes sports and physical activity for Canadian women
19. CAAWS teamed up with this company to develop the Girls@Play program
20. Image concern confronting women and girls
22. First woman to referee an Olympic soccer game
23. Term for condition in which menstrual periods are absent
24. Female health syndrome that includes osteoporosis

Down

1. First woman elected to the Executive of the Canadian Olympic Association
4. Athlete who fought for and won the legal right to participate on boys' teams
7. Official who took away Ben Johnson's ill-gotten gold medal
8. Sport federation that held the Under 19 World Cup championship for women
10. Term that no longer means weak, silent, unthinking waifs
11. Canadian female athlete signed by the Kirkkonummi Salamat team
12. Dubbed the "Queen of Curling" following a gold medal win in the 1998 Nagano Olympic Games
14. Creator of a diploma course in physical education at Margaret Eaton School
16. Contributing factors to this type of eating include low self-esteem and perfectionism
17. Number of women who competed in the first modern Olympic Games
18. Athlete named Canadian Women Athlete for the Half-Century
21. Manon Rheaume made history playing this position

EXERCISE 25.4

Female Role Models in Sports

Successful role models play a critical role in encouraging young athletes to follow their dreams and develop their talent to the fullest. This exercise will introduce you to successful female role models in selected sports.

GREAT CANADIAN SPORTSWOMEN

For each of the following sports, identify a Canadian female role model and describe her achievements. If possible, include a local role model who grew up in or lives in your community. If you were unable to identify a female role model, give possible reasons why this sport lacks female participation.

SPORT	ATHLETE / ACHIEVEMENTS
Alpine skiing	
Baseball	
Basketball	
Cross-country skiing	
Curling	
Cycling	

Diving	
Fencing	
Field hockey	
Figure skating	
Fitness	
Golf	
Hockey	
Sport of choice	
Sport of choice	

EXERCISE 25.5
The Role of Female Athletes

Female sports pioneers have paved the way for the opportunities and successes enjoyed by many Canadian female athletes. This exercise will introduce you to the accomplishments of several of these athletes, as well as their post-career contributions.

CANADIAN WOMEN SPORTS PIONEERS

Choose ten Canadian female athletes from the following list. Using library and Internet resources, research their achievements and fill in the chart below.

- ❑ Elizabeth (Liz) Ashton
- ❑ Angela Bailey
- ❑ Dorothea Beale
- ❑ Marilyn Bell
- ❑ Justine Blainey
- ❑ Debbie Brill
- ❑ Vicki Keith
- ❑ Becky Keller
- ❑ Silken Laumann
- ❑ Carol Anne Letheren
- ❑ Jocelyn Lovell
- ❑ Carolyn Waldo
- ❑ Ethel Catherwood
- ❑ Edmonton Grads
- ❑ The Firth Sisters
- ❑ Sylvie Frechette

- ❑ Elizabeth Manley
- ❑ Alice Milliat
- ❑ Ann Ottenbrite
- ❑ Sharon Wood
- ❑ Nancy Greene
- ❑ Abigail (Abby) Hoffman
- ❑ Sue Holloway
- ❑ Angella Issajenko
- ❑ Lori Kane
- ❑ Ann Peel
- ❑ Manon Rheaume
- ❑ Bobbie (Fanny) Rosenfeld
- ❑ Jamie Sale
- ❑ Barbara Ann Scott
- ❑ Kay Worthington
- ❑ Hayley Wickenheiser

NAME OF ATHLETE	ATHLETIC BACKGROUND	ACHIEVEMENTS AFTER ATHLETIC CAREER
1.		
2.		
3.		

NAME OF ATHLETE	ATHLETIC BACKGROUND	ACHIEVEMENTS AFTER ATHLETIC CAREER
4.		
5.		
6.		
7.		
8.		
9.		
10.		

A ... -square foot ural advertising Toronto's 2008 Olympic bid. CP PHOTO/Aaron Harris.

26
Government Support for Sport and Physical Activity

LEARNING OBJECTIVES

The exercises in this section of the workbook will help to reinforce your knowledge of the following topics covered in the textbook:

- The historical relationship between the Canadian government and sport
- Why sport matters to governments at all levels
- The Mills Report and what it revealed about sport in Canada
- Canada's national Sport Policy and its key points
- How sport is organized in Canada at the various levels of government
- The role of Sport Canada
- The importance of the Canadian Olympic Committee
- The significance of National Sport Organizations (NSOs), Provincial Sport Organizations (PSOs), and Multi-Sport Service Organizations (MSOs)
- The Games of La Francophonie and their importance for the French-speaking world
- Canada's federal sport budget
- How Canada promotes women and youth in sport
- The role of Aboriginal people in Canadian sport
- Sport and the disabled in Canada
- The impact of finance and wagering on Canadian sport

EXERCISE 26.1
Section Quiz

MULTIPLE-CHOICE QUESTIONS

Circle the letter beside the answer that you believe to be correct.

1. **A major report on Canadian sport, released in 1998, was entitled**
   (a) Task Force Report on Sport
   (b) Promoting Physical Activity and Sport
   (c) Sport in Canada
   (d) Canadian Sport Policy

2. **Sport Canada, the major granting agency for sports in Canada, is located within**
   (a) the Athlete Assistance Program
   (b) each provincial and territorial government
   (c) Heritage Canada
   (d) the community of National Games Organizations

3. **The Canadian Olympic Committee is one of the founding partners of**
   (a) Sport Dispute Resolution Centres
   (b) National Sport Organizations
   (c) Provincial Sport Organizations
   (d) Canadian Sports Centres

4. **The Games of La Francophonie are**
   (a) open to Canadian and non-Canadian athletes
   (b) sponsored mainly by government bodies
   (c) a showcase for both sporting and cultural events
   (d) all of the above

5. **Multi-Sport Service Organizations include**
   (a) Athletics Canada
   (b) Canadian Centre for Ethics in Sport
   (c) International Amateur Athletics Federation
   (d) Tennis Canada

6. **The most significant federal program involved with promoting a sports culture in younger age groups is**
   (a) Outreach
   (b) Sport Participation Development Program
   (c) Run Jump Throw
   (d) Kids of Steel

7. **Sporting equipment has been provided to recreation organizations, including many in rural Aboriginal communities, by the**
   (a) UPS Olympic Sports Legacy Program
   (b) Human Resources Development Canada
   (c) Canadian Olympic Association
   (d) Aboriginal Sports Circle

SHORT-ANSWER QUESTIONS

Briefly answer the following questions in the space provided:

1. What is the primary goal of Sport Canada?

2. What is the main responsibility of the Canadian Olympic Committee?

3. What is the new approach developed by the federal government in funding NSOs?

4. Within which Ontario government department is responsibility for sport located?

5. In which international games are medals awarded for both athletic and artistic competition?

6. The Sport Participation Development Program provides financial support to National Sports Organization in which of their efforts?

7. What source of funds provides Sport Canada with 55 percent of its budget?

ESSAY QUESTIONS

On a separate piece of paper, develop a 100-word response to the following questions:

1. State the main recommendations of the *The Mills Report: Sport in Canada* and suggest how they can be implemented.

2. Outline the goals of the Canadian Sport Policy.

3. Describe the various organizations that comprise the "sport community" in Canada and their relationship to one another.

EXERCISE 26.2
Terminology Review

DEFINING KEY TERMS

Briefly explain the meaning of the following key terms:

KEY TERM	DEFINITION
Mills Report	
Sport Dispute Resolution Centre	
Canadian Sport Policy	
Sport Canada	
Canadian Olympic Committee	
Canadian Sport Centres	
National Sport Organizations (NSOs)	
Provincial Sport Organizations (PSOs)	

Multi-Sport Service Organizations (MSOs)	
Games of La Francophonie	
Athlete Assistance Program	
Royal Commission on the Status of Women in Canada	
Sport Participation Development Program	
Aboriginal Sports Circle	
Arctic Winter Games	
Canadian Paralympic Committee	
Special Olympics	
Sports Select and PRO-LINE	
Inter-Provincial Lottery Corporation	

EXERCISE 26.3

The Sport Community in Canada

The sport community in Canada consists of a number of organizations that provide sport programming and activities at the municipal, provincial /territorial, national, and international levels. This exercise will acquaint you with these various levels and some of the organizations within them.

LEVELS OF CANADIAN SPORT

Complete the following chart with a minimum of three examples of each level of sport indicated.

LOCAL	PROVINCIAL	NATIONAL	INTERNATIONAL
Local or community sport clubs	Provincial Games Organizations	National Games Organizations	Major Games Federations
•	•	•	
			•
•	•	•	
			•
•	•	•	
			•
School clubs and teams	Provincial Sport Organizations	National Sport Organizations	International Sport Federations
	•	•	•
•			
	•	•	•
•			
	•	•	•
•			
Post-secondary institutions clubs/teams	Provincial Multi-Sport Organizations	National Multi-Sport Organizations	General Assemblies of International Sports
•	•	•	•
•	•	•	•
•	•	•	•

EXERCISE 26.4

Provincial Sport Organizations

Provincial Sport Organizations (PSOs) play an important role in providing sporting opportunities for Canadians. An understanding of how these organization operate will help you to appreciate the efforts of those involved in them.

THE PSO IN DETAIL

Choose a provincial sport organization (preferably one that you are involved with or one that interests you). Research the organization (using the Internet and making contact with the organization itself) and collect the following information:

Full name of PSO	
When the PSO was founded	
Number of local clubs represented	
Total current individual members	
Is the membership growing?	
Name of president	
Number of full-time staff	
Location of offices	
Website address	
Annual expenditure of the PSO	
Amount of funding received in most recent year	
Current programs offered	
Significant past achievements	

27

Unit 4 Career Choices

Investigate a career in one of the fields covered in Unit 4. Ideally, you should interview someone working in the career for this assignment.

1. Career and description

_____
_____
_____
_____
_____
_____
_____
_____
_____
_____
_____

2. List at least two post-secondary institutions in Ontario and/or Canada that offer programs for this career.

_____
_____
_____
_____

3. Choose one of the above institutions and determine the required courses in the first year of study for this program.

_____
_____
_____
_____
_____
_____
_____
_____
_____

4. What is the total length of the education needed to begin this career? Is an internship or apprenticeship required?

_____
_____
_____
_____
_____

5. What is the average starting salary for this career? What is the top salary? On what do salary increases depend in this career?

_____
_____
_____
_____

6. What is the demand for individuals qualified for this occupation? If possible, provide some employment data to support the answer to this question.

_____
_____
_____
_____
_____
_____
_____

7. List occupational settings where a person with these qualifications could work.

_____
_____
_____
_____
_____

28

Unit 4 Crossword Challenge

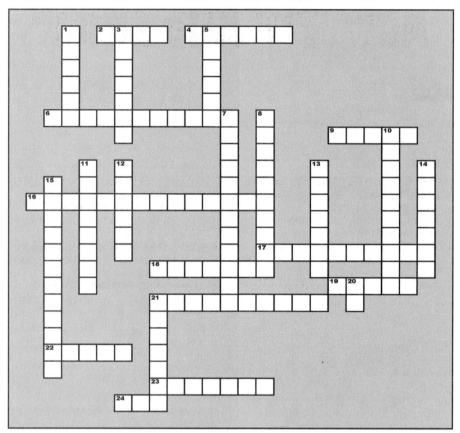

Across

2. Image concern confronting women and girls
4. Status achieved in sport when the same opportunities are equal to everyone
6. Era that produced people equally good at and interested in multiple things
9. Female syndrome that includes disordered eating habits, amenorrhea, and osteoporosis
16. A program created to encourage the Canadian public to become more physically active
17. Federal athlete program that helps athletes meet their living, training, and travel expenses
18. Olympics organized for persons with mental disabilities
19. Report prepared by the Sub-Committee on the Study of Sport in Canada
21. Concept no longer equated with weak, silent, unthinking women
22. Acronym for association founded in 1981 to promote sports and physical activity for women across Canada
23. Athlete who does not receive material rewards from sport
24. League that began its first season in 1917 with five hockey teams

Down

1. Program promoting physical activity for women and girls that provides opportunity for their participation
3. Games originated by the Greeks
5. Canada Games first held here in 1967
7. Relationship in which one party engages in the majority of the effort without receiving a fair share of the results
8. Level of sport organizations that form an intermediary between community and national sport organizations
10. Sports Circle that promotes indigenous games and traditional approaches to amateur sport
11. Level of sport organizations that support athletes in international competitions
12. Winter Games co-hosted in 2002 by Nuuk, Greenland, and Iqaluit, Nunavut
13. Canadian Committee that represents Canada within the IOC
14. Document detailing the goals of the Olympic Movement
15. Series of vigorous exercises and stretches originating in the Victorian era
20. Title of American equal-opportunity legislation affecting female athletes
21. Level of government that developed the Canadian Sport Policy in 2002

UNIT 5

SOCIAL ISSUES IN PHYSICAL ACTIVITY AND SPORT

Notes

29

The (Big) Business of Sport Entertainment

LEARNING OBJECTIVES

The exercises in this section of the workbook will help to reinforce your knowledge of the following topics covered in the textbook:

- The basic principles of sport's relationship to the world of business
- The differences between for-profit and not-for-profit sport
- The fundamental difference between amateur and professional sport
- The reasons behind rising player salaries in professional sport
- The importance of a winning team from an economic perspective
- The role played by the media in the sports-as-entertainment complex
- How television has impacted on sport
- The fundamentals of the sports-as-entertainment industry, including broadcasting rights, player endorsements, the role of sports marketing and promotion
- Key figures in the sport industry: team owners, athletes, agents, and fans
- The role of advertising
- Sports "spin-offs" including replica products, food and beverage sales, alternative use of sports stadiums, charities, and the overall contribution of sport to local economies

EXERCISE 29.1
Section Quiz

MULTIPLE-CHOICE QUESTIONS

Circle the letter beside the answer that you believe to be correct.

1. **Amateur athletes derive compensation for their efforts through**
   (a) player contracts
   (b) endorsement deals
   (c) sale of merchandise and tickets
   (d) none of the above

2. **Formerly for amateurs only, the Olympic Games now permits competition by professional**
   (a) skaters and ice dancers
   (b) hockey and basketball players
   (c) baseball and softball players
   (d) boxers and wrestlers

3. **The largest source of profits for big-business sports teams is**
   (a) athlete endorsements
   (b) ticket sales
   (c) the use of games for the sale of various rights
   (d) concession sales

4. **The WWE "Wrestlemania" events are broadcast as**
   (a) regular over the air telecasts
   (b) conventional cable presentations
   (c) video features
   (d) exclusive pay-per-view engagements

5. **Nike has received criticism for**
   (a) the huge endorsement fees it has paid to celebrity athletes
   (b) the targeting of its marketing towards youth
   (c) the manufacturing of its product in Third World countries
   (d) its advertising at the Atlanta Olympic Games

6. **Which of the following countries participated in the 1980 Olympics, held in Moscow, despite a political boycott?**
   (a) Great Britain
   (b) United States
   (c) Canada
   (d) France

7. **Pro sports teams contribute to their local economy by**
   (a) increasing sales at restaurants and hotels close to stadiums
   (b) employing people in the local community
   (c) paying taxes to the government
   (d) all of the above

SHORT-ANSWER QUESTIONS

Briefly answer the following questions in the space provided:

1. **On what is the distinction between for-profit and not-for-profit sport based?**

2. **What economic concept/theory is used by many to explain the high salaries in professional sports today? Explain.**

3. **The revenue generation of live sports events is similar to what other events?**

4. **What features are offered to viewers as part of the overall sport-as-entertainment package?**

5. **How do broadcasters recoup the massive sums they have paid for broadcasting rights to sporting events? What would happen if this avenue were not open to them?**

6. **Which trend in athlete endorsement and marketing was ushered in by Michael Jordan's huge endorsement contract?**

ESSAY QUESTIONS

On a separate piece of paper, develop a 100-word response to the following questions:

1. **How does a city stand to benefit from hosting the Olympic Games, thereby justifying the enormous cost of preparing a bid for the IOC?**

2. **Compare the "business" of sport in Eastern Europe at the height of the "Cold War," and of Cuba today, with that of North America and Europe.**

3. **Examine the arguments in favour and against the role of a player's agent and explain at least three of them.**

EXERCISE 29.2
Terminology Review

DEFINING KEY TERMS

Briefly explain the meaning of the following key terms:

KEY TERM	DEFINITION
For-profit/not-for-profit sport	
Amateur/professional athletes	
Media	
Sports-as-entertainment industry	
Broadcasting rights	
Endorsement	
Sport franchises	
Player's agent	
Fan loyalty	
Players' strikes	
Stadium concessions	
Charitable activities	

EXERCISE 29.3

Crossword on the Business of Sport Entertainment

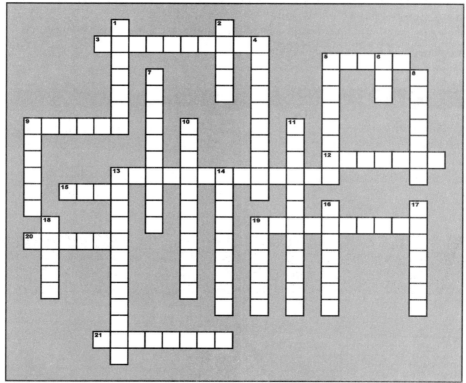

Across

3. Source of financial support for Cuban athletes
5. Negotiator of a player's salary with team owners
9. The other side of the economic theory that posits demand as a major force
12. Products such as team jerseys, supporter banners, scarves
13. Athletes who receive financial rewards for their efforts
15. What consumers must be when it comes to advertising
19. Activities for a cause in which athletes can serve as positive role models
20. Basketball player who refused to comment on Nike's labour practices
21. Along with TV and radio, the twentieth century has seen the birth and growth of sport coverage through this medium

Down

1. Pro teams try to build this among their fans
2. Collective name for television, radio, newspapers, and so on
4. Medium responsible for gradually reshaping the rules of sport
5. Athletes who receive no financial rewards for their efforts
6. Acronym for North American professional sports league with highest average salary
7. Sport organized primarily to make money
8. What the action produced by athletes in big-business sport is known as
9. "The beautiful game" (Pelé)
10. Nowadays, an integral part of professional sport and a major source of revenue
11. Rights to telecast games
13. Runner-up city in the bidding to host the 2010 Winter Olympics
14. High-profile WWE event
16. For many in sport, this is crucial
17. Pro sports teams make money through these streams
18. Golf star who endorsed GM Buick car
19. Former coach who is now the best-known non-player in the hockey world

EXERCISE 29.4

Viewpoints on the Business of Sport

Different individuals and groups benefit from the large sums of money generated by professional sports events. In the following exercise, you will examine how some trends in the "big" business of sport have a varied impact on a number of different groups.

WHO BENEFITS?

In Section 29 of the text, you met several key "players" in the sport-business scene in Canada: athletes and their agents, team owners, broadcasters, and the ticket-buying fans.

In this exercise, you will complete the chart below with one of three responses: "PRO," "CON," or "NR"

(for "not relevant"), depending on whether you think the members of the interest group indicated would be in favour of the sport trend in the right-hand column or opposed to it.

As well, indicate in point form the reason for your choice. One answer is supplied below as an example.

	In general, ticket prices need to be higher	There needs to be more advertising on televised events	Players' unions need to be strengthened	Top players' salaries are still too low
Players/Agents	PRO — expectation that increased revenue will lead to higher player salaries			
Team Owners	PRO — expectation of increased revenue			
Sports fans	CON — becomes harder for average fan to attend events			
Broadcasters	NR — Price of live admission is irrelevant to broadcaster			

EXERCISE 29.5

Changes Inspired in Sport by Television

Of all the various forms of media that have influenced the world of sport, television is the most significant. This exercise will allow you to examine how television has had an impact on the ways in which various sports are played.

SPORTS COVERAGE ON TELEVISION

The following chart lists ten different professional sports, each of which has seen its actual competition changed in a fundamental way by television coverage and/or the advertising that accompanies it. These areas of impact can include rules of sports, the redesign of uniforms and equipment worn by the players, or even the duration and tempo of the sporting event. For each sport indicated, list one such change, and the approximate date at which it occurred. One example is provided below.

Note: Use the Internet, newspapers, magazines, and books to help you fill in the chart below.

SPORT	IMPACT/CHANGE FACTOR	WHEN
1. NBA (Basketball)	"TV Time-outs" held approximately every 4 minutes to allow for more commercials during telecasts	1990s
2. NFL/CFL Football		
3. NHL Hockey		
4. Soccer		
5. Pro Boxing		
6. Pro Golf		
7. Auto Racing		
8. Pro Baseball		
9. Pro Tennis		
10. Track and field		

Jody Holden, 2000. CP Photo/Scott Grant.

30

School and Community Sport Programs

LEARNING OBJECTIVES

The exercises in this section of the workbook will help to reinforce your knowledge of the following topics covered in the textbook:

- Historical trends in the development of sport programs in Canadian schools and communities
- The rise of physical education as a subject in Canadian schools
- Early Canadian school and/or community sport pioneers
- Contemporary trends in Canadian school physical education
- Various organizations that support school physical education and sport in Canada
- The significance of sport scholarships for Canadian high-school athletes
- The basic structure of community sport programs in Canada
- Various notable Canadian sport leagues and clubs for youth
- Health and Physical Education Associations across Canada
- The growth of the YMCA and YWCA in Canada
- Significant community sport initiatives in Canada
- The role of recreational programs in helping "at-risk" youth
- How physical activity can improve overall health and personal development
- How sport helps in creating social networks
- Notable Canadians who have raised awareness of social issues through sport
- The health, social, and economic benefits of large-scale sport programs

EXERCISE 30.1
Section Quiz

MULTIPLE-CHOICE QUESTIONS

Circle the letter beside the answer that you believe to be correct.

1. **In elite English private schools, physical education was**
   (a) a vital part of every student's life
   (b) recognized as inherently valuable
   (c) a legitimate academic course
   (d) mainly a means for training military commanders

2. **In 1910, physical education in Canadian public schools**
   (a) was taught by retired military officers
   (b) featured drills, calisthenics, and gymnastics
   (c) prepared the masses for a lifetime of hard work
   (d) all of the above

3. **An extensive plan for public education was developed in 1844 by**
   (a) Egerton Ryerson
   (b) Thomas Arnold
   (c) Lord Strathcona
   (d) Matthew Arnold

4. **According to the Canadian Association for Health, Physical Education, Recreation and Dance (CAHPERD), what is the recommended weekly minimum of physical education instruction in schools?**
   (a) 75 minutes
   (b) 150 minutes
   (c) 250 minutes
   (d) 100 minutes

5. **The main focus of amateur hockey leagues is**
   (a) learning team skills
   (b) teaching athletes to have fun
   (c) improving the competitive level of the sport
   (d) supporting amateur hockey in Canada

6. **The PRYDE program features which sport to combat increasing youth inactivity?**
   (a) boxing
   (b) basketball
   (c) judo
   (d) wrestling

7. **At what activity do Canadian children spend most of their time?**
   (a) watching television
   (b) sleeping
   (c) surfing the Net
   (d) reading

SHORT-ANSWER QUESTIONS

Briefly answer the following questions in the space provided:

1. **How was the curriculum of Rugby College in England affected by its headmaster from 1828 to 1842?**

2. **What is the goal of the Canadian Intramural Recreation Association?**

3. **What factors must be considered by athletes who have been offered a sport scholarship?**

4. **What are the four key areas that organizers of community programs must consider. Why?**

5. **Name four major initiatives undertaken by the YMCA since its inception.**

6. **What is the most important feature of drop-in centres?**

7. **How many minutes of physical exercise do Canadians need per day to enjoy optimal health benefits?**

ESSAY QUESTIONS

On a separate piece of paper, develop a 100-word response to the following questions:

1. **Discuss the effect of budget cuts in the 1990s on physical education programs in schools.**

2. **Describe the role and work of the Canadian School Sport Federation.**

3. **Outline the issues that organizers of community programs must consider.**

EXERCISE 30.2
Terminology Review

DEFINING KEY TERMS

Briefly explain the meaning of the following key terms:

KEY TERM	DEFINITION
Muscular Christianity	
Canadian Association for Health, Physical Education, Recreation and Dance (CAHPERD)	
Canadian Intramural Recreation Association	
Canadian School Sport Federation	
Coaching Association of Canada (CAC)	
Sport Leadership Program	

Canadian Hockey Association (CHA)	
Community recreation centres	
Ophea (Ontario Physical and Health Education Association)	
Young Men's Christian Association (YMCA)	
Drop-in centre programs	
Midnight Basketball League	
Grass Roots Canada Basketball	
ESTEEM Team	
Quality of life	

EXERCISE 30.3

Developing a Community Sport League

There are many organizational aspects to running school- and community-based sport programs. The following exercise will give you an opportunity to work through many of the challenges faced by sport organizations at this level.

ORGANIZATION IN ACTION

Begin by forming groups of students (3 to 5). Imagine that your group has volunteered to act as the executive committee for a new soccer league for children thirteen years of age and under in your community. The league has been given $5,000 through a municipal grant to begin operations. You will also be able to collect registration fees from your players.

Your task is to begin to organize the league's first year of play. Some of the information below will be for organizational purposes; in some cases, you will be required to input dollar figures. Also, you will need to decide which age divisions will incorporate mixed boys and girls play, and which will be single-sex only.

Finally, on the next page, complete an income and expense budget for the first year. Keep in mind that your expenses must not exceed what you take in. It is also a good idea to have some money left over for the following year's executive to work with. In some instances, research will be required (e.g., to discover the cost of field rental, insurance, and equipment in your community).

KICK-OFF YOUTH SOCCER LEAGUE: PREPARATION NOTES

President	
Vice-President	
Secretary	
Total target registration (Boys/Girls)	
What is the league's "philosophy" (e.g., "fun league" or "competitive league")? How will this philosophy be articulated to players and coaches?	
Number of age divisions and age breakdown (e.g., under-5; under-7; etc.) for girls-only, boys only, and mixed?	
How will the league be promoted and advertised to prospective players and their parents?	
Will officials be involved on a voluntary basis (e.g., parents and coaches) or will paid officials be required (e.g., referees)? If paid officials are needed, what is the cost per division?	
Cost of insurance for league?	
Cost of field(s) rental?	
Cost of uniforms purchase?	
Costs of equipment (e.g., balls, nets, etc.)?	
Registration fee per player: Are basic player photograph costs included in registration fee? Cost of trophies, awards to players? Cost of year-end party? Cost of coach/volunteer "appreciation night?"	
Cost (if any) of registering league with larger organization (e.g., Canadian Soccer Association)?	
What policies exist within the community recreation structure that will govern league play? (e.g., city-wide facilities policy on zero-tolerance for violence)?	
Other considerations	

SAMPLE INCOME AND EXPENDITURE STATEMENT

The income statement below is from a real community tennis club for the year 2002. Use it to model your own expected "income and expenditure" statement for a hypothetical local club. Cross out the expenditure items that do not apply and substitute new expenditure items and dollar figures as necessary for the club you are setting up.

If you wish to do this in a spreadsheet program, the sample below (which you can modify as required) is available at: www.thompsonbooks.com/hpe/incomesample.xls

---

COMMUNITY TENNIS CLUB

Statement of Income and Expenses and Members' Equity
For The Year Ended September 30, 2002

	(SAMPLE) 2002 $	
Income		
Membership fees	26,506.00	_____
Interest	798.00	
Other income	-	
	27,304.00	_____
Expenses		
Audit fee	-	
Bank charges	76.00	_____
Court steward fees	1,883.00	_____
Junior program	1,783.00	_____
Tennis balls	1,573.00	_____
Team expenses	170.00	_____
Trophies, prizes and gifts	-	_____
Repairs and maintenance	147.00	_____
Social events	3,323.00	_____
Insurance	1,148.00	_____
Ontario Tennis Association	-	_____
Postage and printing	826.00	_____
Telephone	-	_____
Shoe tags	442.00	_____
Meetings	-	_____
Website	88.00	_____
	11,459.00	
Excess of income over expenses	15,845.00	_____
Court renovations	56,817.00	_____
Excess of expenses over income	**(40,972.00)**	_____
Members' Equity		
Equity, beginning of year	77,353.00	_____
Equity, end of year	**36,381.00**	_____

EXERCISE 30.4

American Sport Scholarships for Canadians

For Canadian high-school athletes, there are a number of important issues to consider when offered a sports scholarship to a university or college in the United States. The following exercise requires you to conduct research into the nature of these scholarships.

SPORT SCHOLARSHIP INVESTIGATION

Choose four sports in which sports scholarships are available at U.S. colleges and universities. Use the Internet (two important sites to visit are the official sites of the National Collegiate Athletic Association at www.ncaa.org and www.ncaasports.com to do your research) and complete the chart below.

One entry using the sport of tennis has been completed as an example.

Sport	Number of NCAA Division One schools who compete in this sport (men and women)	Number of scholarships available in NCAA competition (men and women)	Three Canadian athletes who currently compete on scholarship, their hometown, and their school affiliation	Current NCAA Division One champion school in this sport (men and women)
Tennis	Men: 754 Women: 892 Total:1636	Men: 274 Women: 316 Total 590	Rahim Esmail (Victoria, B.C.) — University of Kentucky Oscar Chow (Vancouver, B.C.) — Columbia University (New York) Sanja Bajin (King City, Ont.) — Harvard University (Cambridge, Mass.)	Men: University of Illinois Women: University of Florida
Sport 1: _____				

Sport	Number of NCAA Division One schools who compete in this sport (men and women)	Number of scholarships available in NCAA competition (men and women)	Three Canadian athletes who currently compete on scholarship, their hometown, and their school affiliation	Current NCAA Division One champion school in this sport (men and women)
Sport 2: _____				
Sport 3: _____				
Sport 4: _____				

31
Social and Ethical Problems in Sport

LEARNING OBJECTIVES

The exercises in this section of the workbook will help to reinforce your knowledge of the following topics covered in the textbook:

- The role that ethical and social considerations play in sport at all levels
- How Canada has developed its own strategy for the development of a policy in ethical conduct in sport
- The role of violence and aggression in sport
- Various modes of sports violence
- The numerous ways it is possible to cheat at sport, including recruitment violations, corruption of officials, and bribery
- The use of drugs in sport, including the history of drug use, drug-testing "mistakes," the World Anti-Doping Agency, and the use of "recreational" drugs
- The significance of tobacco and alcohol sponsorships for sporting events
- Gambling and its impact on sport

EXERCISE 31.1
Section Quiz

MULTIPLE-CHOICE QUESTIONS

Circle the letter beside the answer that you believe to be correct.

1. **The Ottawa-based Canadian Centre for Ethics in Sport is responsible for**
   (a) co-creating the Canadian Strategy for Ethical Conduct in Sport
   (b) administering Canada's drug-free sport policy
   (c) policy making in the promotion of drug-free, fair, and ethical sport
   (d) all of the above

2. **Factors that increase the likelihood of violence in sports include:**
   (a) high scoring games
   (b) higher athletes salaries
   (c) decrease in ticket sales
   (d) fans having unrealistically high expectations of a team

3. **During the 2002 World Cup, a Korean man did this to support his nation's soccer team.**
   (a) lit himself on fire
   (b) went on a hunger strike
   (c) chained himself to the stadium
   (d) none of the above

4. **In Canada, in order for athletes to retain amateur status, they cannot**
   (a) deny any incentives offered
   (b) be over fifteen
   (c) accept any money or promised payment
   (d) refuse coaching assistance from the government

5. **When attempting to persuade student-athletes to accept scholarships, coaches sometimes commit recruiting violations that can include**
   (a) free hotel rooms
   (b) money
   (c) gifts
   (d) all of the above

6. **Which of the following have been proven to enhance athletic performance?**
   (a) cocaine
   (b) heroin
   (c) marijuana
   (d) none of the above

7. **In Ontario, betting on sports for adult sports fans is**
   (a) illegal
   (b) legal and unregulated
   (c) illegal but generally tolerated
   (d) legal but highly regulated

SHORT-ANSWER QUESTIONS

Briefly answer the following questions in the space provided:

1. **Why was the Canadian Strategy for Ethical Conduct in Sport created ?**

2. **What action did the NHL take against Marty McSorley for his attack against Donald Brashear?**

3. **What is the worst example of soccer fan violence in recent times?**

4. **What do the many different ways to cheat include?**

5. **What honour did the members of the Asahi baseball team, interned during the Second World War, recently receive?**

6. **According to the head of the CCES, Paul Melia, who is ultimately responsible for how an athlete does on a urine test?**

ESSAY QUESTIONS

On a separate piece of paper, develop a 100-word response to the following questions:

1. **Outline the goals of the Canadian Strategy for Ethical Conduct in Sport.**

2. **Discuss why bribery has entered the bidding process for the right to host the Olympic Games.**

3. **Summarize the history of steroid use in athletic competition.**

EXERCISE 31.2
Terminology Review

DEFINING KEY TERMS

Briefly explain the meaning of the following key terms:

KEY TERM	DEFINITION
Canadian Strategy for Ethical Conduct in Sport	
Canadian Centre for Ethics in Sport	
Instrumental aggression	
Hostile aggression	
Cheating	
Recruiting violations	
Corruption of judges and officials	
World Anti-Doping Agency	
World Anti-Doping Code	
Athlete's Passport Program	
"Recreational" drug use	
Sports gambling	

EXERCISE 31.3

Crossword on Social and Ethical Problems in Sport

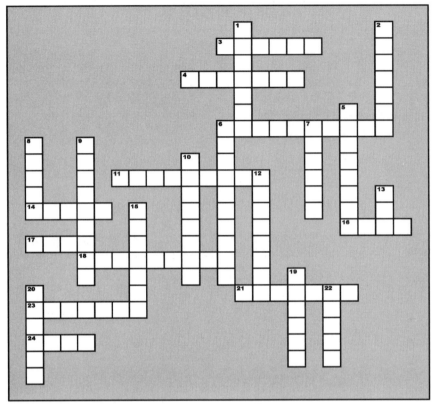

Across

3. Spectator violence among the fans of this sport is a large problem in England
4. Pete Rose of the Cincinnati Reds was banned from baseball for life because of this
6. Violations intended to entice players to choose a particular university
11. Because of their decision-making responsibilities, they are often the target of fan violence
14. Tennis player stabbed by fan of Steffi Graf
16. Along with Pelletier, this skater maintained dignity in a corrupt judging case
17. Toronto Maple Leaf renowned for fighting
18. Altering this necessity of sport is a form of cheating
21. Soccer player subsequently murdered for scoring on his own goal in World Cup soccer
23. "Recreational" substance often used by athletes to ease stress
24. Acronym for Canadian organization that develops policies on ethical issues in sport

Down

1. Type of aggression featuring the deliberate intent to harm another player
2. Many believe this needs to be reformed in many sports
5. In baseball, these players cheat by changing the flight properties of the ball
6. Canadian athlete stripped of his gold medal for marijuana use
7. A difficult thing for officials to determine when a player has been injured by another
8. Nine-time Olympic gold medallist accused of failing a drug test at 1988 U.S. Olympic Trials
9. Large sponsors of sporting events
10. Criminal charges were brought against this Bruins' player who smashed Donald Brashear over the head with his stick
12. The side effects of these drugs was unknown until the late 1950s
13. Acronym of professional sports league that opposes drug testing of players
15. Conduct that must be taught universally and from a young age
19. The first athletes charged with this were European swimmers in the 1860s
20. Rule-breakers have traditionally "succeeded" in this racing series
22. Team composed of Japanese-Canadians that came to dominate in the Pacific Northwest

EXERCISE 31.4

Ethical Issues in Sport

A wide range of ethical considerations emerge every day on the world sporting stage. In the following exercise, you will be asked to research current "real life" examples of these ethical issues.

SPORT ETHICS RESEARCH

Using any media outlet that reports regularly on sport, research five recent examples of an ethical controversy in the world of sport, and complete the chart below.

Sources for your research can include:

- any major Canadian newspaper (such as the *Globe and Mail*, *Toronto Star*, *National Post*, and so on) or even foreign newspapers (note that most newspapers have complete editions online);
- any sports magazine (such as *Sports Illustrated* or *The Hockey News*);
- any news broadcast on TV or radio that includes sports highlights;
- any live broadcast on TV or radio of a sporting event.

One fictional sample entry is provided below.

MEDIA STORY	SUMMARY OF EVENTS AND ETHICAL CONSIDERATION IN QUESTION
"Sosa goes off half-corked: Cubs star caught with illegal bat in game against Cards" *Globe and Mail*, July 5, 2003, A6.	Baseball player Sammy Sosa found to be using illegal bat containing cork to aid hitting for distance **Issue**: The use of illegal equipment to gain advantage
1.	
2.	
3.	
4.	
5.	

EXERCISE 31.5

Drug Violations in International Sport

Many high-profile athletes have been caught using banned performance-enhancing substances. This has profoundly affected (and in some cases, ended) their sports careers. In the following exercise, you will be asked to investigate four such cases.

DRUG VIOLATION RESEARCH

Using a variety of sources, fill in the following table with as much information as possible on five athletes who have been caught using performance-enhancing substances in the sports listed below.

It is recommended that you do a quick review of Section 11 of the text (Performance-Enhancing Substances and Techniques) before completing the chart. One entry has been completed as an example.

SPORT	ATHLETE/COUNTRY	EVENT/DATE TESTED POSITIVE	RESULT OF TEST (ACTION TAKEN)	SUMMARY OF CAREER AFTER TESTING POSITIVE
1. Track and field (men)	Ben Johnson (Canada)	1988 Seoul Olympics, positive test came after win in men's 100 metre in world-record time	Stripped of gold medal; banned from sport for 3 years; also stripped of earlier world record	Attempted comeback; failed drug test again in 1993 and banned for life from track and field
2. Track and field (women)				
3. Weightlifting (men)				
4. Swimming (women)				
5. Any other sport of your choice (men or women)				

32
Unit 5 Career Choices

Investigate a career in one of the fields covered in Unit 5. Ideally, you should interview someone working in the career for this assignment.

1. Career and description

_____

_____

_____

_____

_____

_____

_____

_____

_____

_____

_____

2. List at least two post-secondary institutions in Ontario and/or Canada that offer programs for this career.

_____

_____

_____

3. Choose one of the above institutions and determine the required courses in the first year of study for this program.

_____

_____

_____

_____

_____

_____

_____

_____

_____

4. What is the total length of the education needed to begin this career? Is an internship or apprenticeship required?

_____

_____

_____

_____

5. What is the average starting salary for this career? What is the top salary? On what do salary increases depend in this career?

_____

_____

_____

_____

6. What is the demand for individuals qualified for this occupation? If possible, provide some employment data to support the answer to this question.

_____

_____

_____

_____

_____

_____

7. List occupational settings where a person with these qualifications could work.

_____

_____

_____

_____

33

Unit 5 Crossword Challenge

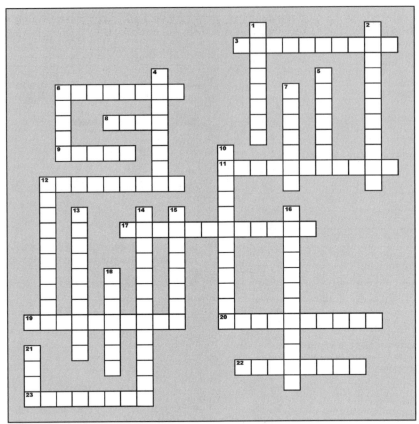

Across

3. Olympic judges and officials may be guilty of this
6. Type of Christianity coined by Thomas Hughes
8. Their loyalty is the central asset of a sports franchise
9. Negotiator of a player's salary with team owners
11. The appearance of athletes in advertisements for products
12. Recreation centres that offer a common meeting ground
17. Rights to telecast games
19. Violations intended to entice players to choose a particular university
20. What the Coaching Association of Canada offers at various levels
22. Attempt to gain an unfair advantage in training or in competition
23. Athletes who receive no financial rewards for their efforts

Down

1. Canadian association that offers programs for training and certification of coaches
2. Food and beverage venues in stadiums
4. Athlete's program that allows athlete's to demonstrate their commitment to keeping sports clean of drug use
5. Type of aggression marked by the deliberate intent to harm another player
6. Collective term for television, radio, newspapers, and so on
7. Acronym for the Ottawa-based national charitable organization that promotes exercise in schools
10. The use of such drugs as marijuana, cocaine, or heroin
12. Activities in which athletes can serve as positive role models by raising funds
13. Canadian recreation association that seeks to reduce physical inactivity through sport in education
14. Athletes who receive financial rewards for their efforts
15. In Canada, this aspect of sport is legal but highly regulated
16. Type of aggression in which injury of another player is a side effect
18. Conduct promoted by the Canadian Centre for Ethics in Sport
21. Founded by Englishman George Williams in the 1840s

Appendices

Age (years): 15-19

Measures	BMI		SO5S		WG		SO2S	
Gender	M	F	M	F	M	F	M	F
	18	17	25	36	67	61	11	13
	19	18	27	40	68	63	12	14
	19	19	28	43	64	64	13	16
	20	19	29	46	70	65	13	17
	20	19	31	49	72	65	14	18
	20	20	32	51	72	66	15	19
	21	20	33	54	73	67	15	20
	21	20	35	56	74	67	16	21
	21	21	36	58	75	68	17	22
	22	21	38	61	76	68	17	23
	22	22	40	63	77	69	18	24
	22	22	42	66	78	70	19	26
	22	22	44	69	79	70	21	27
	23	23	47	72	80	71	22	29
	23	23	51	77	81	72	24	31
	24	24	54	83	82	72	27	33
	25	25	61	89	84	74	28	37
	26	26	69	97	88	77	32	42
	28	28	82	116	95	81	42	49

Age (years): 20-29

	M	F	M	F	M	F	M	F
	19	18	26	37	71	61	13	13
	20	18	29	40	73	63	14	14
	21	19	30	43	75	64	16	16
	21	19	32	46	76	65	17	17
	22	20	34	49	77	65	18	18
	22	20	36	51	78	66	19	19
	22	20	38	53	79	66	20	20
	23	21	40	56	80	67	21	21
	23	21	43	58	81	68	23	22
	23	21	46	60	82	69	25	23
	24	22	49	63	83	70	27	24
	24	22	52	65	84	71	28	26
	25	22	55	69	85	72	30	27
	25	23	58	72	86	73	32	29
	26	23	62	76	87	75	35	31
	27	24	68	81	89	77	38	33
	27	25	74	86	91	78	41	36
	28	26	82	95	93	81	46	42
	30	28	94	111	97	86	54	48

*Based on data from the Canada Fitness Survey, 1981

**BMI: Body Mass Index = Body Weight (kg) divided by Height (m)

SO5S: Sum of (five) Skinfolds (mm) = Triceps + Biceps + Subscapular + Illiac Crest + Medial Calf

WG: Waist Girth (cm)

SO2S: Sum of (two) Trunk Skinfolds (mm) = Subscapular + Illiac Crest

Estimated health benefit zones according to trends in morbidity and mortality data.

Source: The Canadian Physical Activity Fitness and Lifestyle Appraisal: CSEP's Plan for Healthy Active Living, 2nd edition. 1998. Reprinted with permission from the Canadian Society for Exercise Physiology.

PART ONE: DETERMINATION OF HEALTH BENEFIT ZONES

Scoring of Body Composition Assessments

BMI and SO5S healthy	8 points	WG healthy and SO2S healthy	8 points
BMI unhealthy and SO5S healthy	8 points	WG healthy and SO2S unhealthy	4 points
BMI healthy and SO5S unhealthy	3 points	WG unhealthy and SO2S unhealthy	2 points
BMI unhealthy and SO5S unhealthy	0 points	WG unhealthy and SO2S healthy	0 points

Corresponding Health Benefit Zones for Healthy Body Composition

16 points	Excellent
12 points	Very Good
7-11 points	Good
4-5 points	Fair
0-3 points	Needs Improvement

PART TWO: BENEFITS OF HEALTHY BODY COMPOSITION

Health Benefit Zone

Excellent	Your body composition falls within a range that is generally associated with optimal health benefits.
Very Good	Your body composition falls within a range that is generally associated with considerable health benefits.
Good	Your body composition falls within a range that is generally associated with many health benefits.
Fair	Your body composition falls within a range that is generally associated with some health benefits, but also some health risks. *Progressing from here into the GOOD zone is a very significant step to increasing the health benefits associated with your body composition.*
Needs Improvement	Your body composition falls within a range that is generally associated with considerable health risks. *Try to achieve and maintain a healthy body composition by enjoying regular physical activity and healthy eating.*

Source: The Canadian Physical Activity Fitness and Lifestyle Appraisal: CSEP's Plan for Healthy Active Living, 2nd edition. 1998. Reprinted with permission from the Canadian Society for Exercise Physiology.

APPENDIX C: Starting Stage by Age and Gender		
	Starting Stage	
Age	Males	Females
60-69	1	1
50-59	2	1
40-49	3	2
30-39	3	3
20-29	4	3
15-19	4	3

Source: The Canadian Physical Activity Fitness and Lifestyle Appraisal: CSEP's Plan for Healthy Active Living, 2nd edition. 1998. Reprinted with permission from the Canadian Society for Exercise Physiology.

APPENDIX D: Ceiling Post-Exercise Heart Rates

Age	Heart Rate* 10-second count	Heart Rate* Monitor reading	Age	Heart Rate* 10-second count	Heart Rate* Monitor reading
15	29	174	43	25	150
16	28	173	44	25	150
17	28	173	45	25	149
18	28	172	46	24	148
19	28	171	47	24	147
20	28	170	48	24	146
21	28	169	49	24	145
22	28	168	50	24	145
23	28	167	51	24	144
24	28	167	52	24	143
25	27	166	53	23	142
26	27	165	54	23	141
27	27	164	55	23	140
28	27	163	56	23	139
29	27	162	57	23	139
30	27	162	58	23	138
31	27	161	59	23	137
32	26	160	60	22	136
33	26	159	61	22	135
34	26	158	62	22	134
35	26	157	63	22	133
36	26	156	64	22	133
37	26	156	65	22	132
38	26	155	66	22	131
39	25	154	67	21	130
40	25	153	68	21	129
41	25	152	69	21	128
42	25	151			

*85% of predicted maximum (220-age). Determined for each age and to balance accuracy and safety, rounding of 10 sec. counts was determined as follows: less than or equal to 0.8, round down and greater than 0.8, round up.
Source: The Canadian Physical Activity Fitness and Lifestyle Appraisal: CSEP's Plan for Healthy Active Living, 2nd edition. 1998. Reprinted with permission from the Canadian Society for Exercise Physiology.

APPENDIX E: Determination of Health Benefit Zone from Aerobic Fitness Score

Age (years): 15-19		
Zone	Male	Female
Excellent	574+	490+
Very Good	524-573	437-489
Good	488-523	395-436
Fair	436-487	386-394
Needs improvement	<436	<368
Age (years): 20-29		
Zone	Male	Female
Excellent	556+	472+
Very Good	506-555	420-471
Good	472-505	378-419
Fair	416-471	350-377
Needs improvement	<416	<350

Source: The Canadian Physical Activity Fitness and Lifestyle Appraisal: CSEP's Plan for Healthy Active Living, 2nd edition. 1998. Reprinted with permission from the Canadian Society for Exercise Physiology.

APPENDIX F: Health Benefits of Aerobic Fitness

Health Benefit Zone	
Excellent	Your aerobic fitness falls within a range that is generally associated with optimal health benefits.
Very Good	Your aerobic fitness falls within a range that is generally associated with considerable health benefits.
Good	Your aerobic fitness falls within a range that is generally associated with many health benefits.
Fair	Your aerobic fitness falls within a range that is generally associated with some health benefits but also some health risks. *Progressing from the GOOD zone and beyond requires accumulating 30 minutes or more of vigorous physical activity over the course of most days of the week. This is a **very significant** step to increasing the health benefits from aerobic fitness.*
Needs Improvement	Your aerobic fitness falls within a range that is generally associated with considerable health risks. *Try to accumulate 30 minutes or more of moderate-intensity physical activity over the course of most days of the week.*

Source: The Canadian Physical Activity Fitness and Lifestyle Appraisal: CSEP's Plan for Healthy Active Living, 2nd edition. 1998. Reprinted with permission from the Canadian Society for Exercise Physiology.

APPENDIX G: Healthy Musculoskeletal Fitness: Norms and Health Benefit Zones by Age Groups and Gender

	Grip Strength* (kg)		Push-Ups (#)		Trunk Fwd Flexion (cm)		Partial Curl-Up (#)		Vertical Jump (cm)	
Age (years): 15-19										
Zone	M	F	M	F	M	F	M	F	M	F
Excellent	≥113	≥71	≥39	≥33	≥39	≥43	25	25	≥51	≥37
Very Good	103-112	64-70	29-38	25-32	34-38	38-42	23-24	23-24	37-50	29-36
Good	95-102	59-63	23-28	18-24	29-33	34-37	21-22	21-22	27-36	22-28
Fair	84-94	54-58	18-22	12-17	24-28	29-33	16-20	16-20	18-26	15-21
Needs Improvement	≤83	≤53	≤17	≤11	≤23	≤28	≤15	≤15	≤17	≤14
Age (years): 20-29										
Zone	M	F	M	F	M	F	M	F	M	F
Excellent	≥124	≥71	≥36	≥30	≥40	≥41	25	25	≥56	≥40
Very Good	113-122	65-70	29-35	21-29	34-39	37-40	23-24	23-24	39-55	28-39
Good	106-112	61-64	22-28	15-20	30-33	33-36	21-22	19-22	30-38	20-27
Fair	97-105	55-60	17-21	10-14	25-29	28-32	13-20	13-18	21-29	15-21
Needs Improvement	≤96	≤54	≤16	≤9	≤24	≤27	≤12	≤12	≤20	≤14

*Combined right and left hand. *Source: The Canadian Physical Activity Fitness and Lifestyle Appraisal: CSEP's Plan for Healthy Active Living,* 2nd edition. 1998. Reprinted with permission from the Canadian Society for Exercise Physiology.

APPENDIX H: Health Benefit Zones by Age Groups and Gender for Leg Power* from Vertical Jump

Age	15-19		20-29		30-39		40-49		50-59		60-69	
Zone	M	F	M	F	M	F	M	F	M	F	M	F
Excellent	≥104	≥74	≥121	≥78	≥120	≥74	≥113	≥72	≥105	≥71	≥98	≥64
Very Good	88-103	67-73	102-120	65-77	102-119	64-73	96-112	60-71	93-104	63-70	84-97	56-63
Good	73-87	58-66	89-101	56-64	87-101	56-63	81-95	56-59	76-92	57-62	75-83	53-55
Fair	61-72	51-57	74-88	52-55	70-86	51-55	73-80	52-55	68-75	54-56	67-74	49-52
Needs Improvement	≤60	≤50	≤73	≤51	≤69	≤50	≤72	≤51	≤67	≤53	≤66	≤48

*Leg power in kg-m/sec. *Source: The Canadian Physical Activity Fitness and Lifestyle Appraisal: CSEP's Plan for Healthy Active Living,* 2nd edition. 1998. Reprinted with permission from the Canadian Society for Exercise Physiology.

APPENDIX I: Benefits of Healthy Musculoskeletal Fitness

Health Benefit Zone	
Excellent	Your musculoskeletal fitness falls within a range that is generally associated with optimal health benefits.
Very Good	Your musculoskeletal fitness falls within a range that is generally associated with considerable health benefits.
Good	Your musculoskeletal fitness falls within a range that is generally associated with many health benefits.
Fair	Your musculoskeletal fitness falls within a range that is generally associated with some health benefits but also some health risks. *Progressing from the GOOD zone and beyond requires utilizing your major muscle groups more vigorously against resistance two to three times per week. This is a **very significant** step to increasing the health benefits from musculoskeletal fitness.*
Needs improvement	Your musculoskeletal fitness falls within a range that is generally associated with considerable health risks. *Try to utilize your major muscle groups against resistance at least twice per week.*

Source: The Canadian Physical Activity Fitness and Lifestyle Appraisal: CSEP's Plan for Healthy Active Living, 2nd edition. 1998. Reprinted with permission from the Canadian Society for Exercise Physiology.